International Terrorism

International Terrorism

An Introduction to the Concepts and Actors

Donna M. Schlagheck
Wright State University

Lexington Books
D.C. Heath and Company/Lexington, Massachusetts/Toronto

Library of Congress Cataloging-in-Publication Data

Schlagheck, Donna M.
   International terrorism.

   Includes index.
   1. Terrorism. I. Title.
HV6431.S33   1988   303.6′25   86-46322
ISBN 0-669-15432-0 (alk. paper)
ISBN 0-669-15454-7 (pbk. : alk. paper)

Published simultaneously in Canada
Printed in the United States of America
Casebound International Standard Book Number: 0-669-15452-0
Paperbound International Standard Book Number: 0-669-15454-7
Library of Congress Catalog Card Number 86-46322

The paper used in this publication meets the minimum requirements of American National Standard for Information Sciences—Permanence of Paper for Printed Library Materials, ANSI Z39.48-1984. ∞™

88 89 90 91 92   8 7 6 5 4 3 2 1

Contents

Acknowledgements

I am indebted to the College of Liberal Arts Research Committee at Wright State University for its valuable assistance and support. I am personally indebted to many people who have helped me to see more clearly and think more deeply. And I wish to thank Spencer Hall and Joanne Ballmann for providing the very special support that all completed manuscripts require.

Preface

The last twenty years have witnessed a groundswell of interest in terrorism among the public and universities alike. The Weather Underground's bombing of the U.S. Senate men's room, hijackings to Cuba and the Middle East, the attack on Israeli athletes at the 1972 Munich Olympic Games, and the detention of Americans at the Tehran Embassy, 1979–1981, laid the bases for public curiosity and scholarly investigation. As this book goes to press, incidents of terrorism in the Occupied Territories and in Northern Ireland again have claimed world attention. Scholars will continue to study terrorism and produce sophisticated analyses of the phenomenon, but for the undergraduate or interested citizen, that scholarship represents a barrier to understanding terrorism. The sizable body of scholarship on terrorism, much of it dating from the late 1960s, has not been integrated or synthesized so that it can be presented to the "curious but uninitiated." The technical and often highly specialized studies of terrorism do not address the basic, conceptual questions that should be addressed, including "What is terrorism? Who employs terrorism? Why? What are the remedies?" This book was designed expressly to fill that void.

This book was written for students in a variety of courses, and it focuses on the recurring questions about terrorism, politics, and violence using case illustrations. As supplementary reading in an introductory or intermediate international relations course, in a comparative politics course, or in a more specialized course focusing on political violence or terrorism, this book will help illuminate the basic concepts and issues in international terrorism. It is useful as specialized reading in a world politics course, or to establish the framework for a terrorism seminar.

The book is written without technical jargon or an emphasis on weapons. It focuses on actors, concepts, and issues and is suitable for students at many levels. Its goal is to make scholarship more accessible and more widely understood. In the age of terrorism, it is more important than ever that we investigate and teach about political violence if our civil society is to endure.

1
Introduction: What Is Terrorism? Why Study It?

What Is Terrorism?

> Terrorism is the deliberate and systematic murder, maiming and menacing of the innocent to inspire fear for political ends.[1]
>
> Terrorism is unorthodox and unexpected violence designed to coerce and intimidate rather than to destroy an opponent. It is meant to influence the political behavior of adversaries by attacking and threatening targets that possess symbolic rather than material significance. Consequently, its victims are often civilians, but terrorism need not necessarily cause casualties.[2]

Terrorism is now one of the paradoxes of our times. Its threat is as pervasive as nuclear war, but its victims are relatively few in number. Nonetheless, its consequences are publicized widely in excruciating detail. Terrorism affects individuals, societies, governments, and interstate relations. It is both deadly and frightening. Despite all this, and all the studies of terrorism, there is no agreement on how to define it. Experts, governments, and the United Nations wrestle with the problem of defining terrorism so they can get on with the business of combatting it, but no consensus emerges on how to define terrorism. More than one hundred definitions (including those above) have been proposed[3] and the number continues to grow. Among the definitions there is some agreement on the elements that comprise terrorism. By looking at those components a clearer picture of terrorism emerges.

Terrorism Involves the Use of Violence or the Threat of Violence.

Violence consistently appears in definitions of terrorism. Violence has three sides:

a. The intent to do harm or cause injury,

    b. The actions that produce harm or injury (such as bombing, assassination, hijacking, and kidnapping), and

    c. The perception or understanding of the victims who are the targets and witnesses of the violence.

The violence of terrorism is not accidental. The victims of a terrible automobile crash are frightened and injured, but their fear and injury are different from the fright and harm created by the bombing of a busy department store or restaurant. Threatening or causing terrorist violence is an intentional act. It is done with a purpose in mind, and that purpose is meant to be communicated to the people on the receiving end of the violence and to those looking on.

The Violence of Terrorism Is Unpredictable.

Terrorism's threat is great because of the element of surprise and unpredictability in terrorist attacks. Where and when the attack will occur, who the target will be, how the strike will be carried out—all these questions remain a mystery until the terrorist acts. Fear of the unknown and the anticipation of violence heighten the anxiety surrounding terrorist violence and increase its impact. Because terrorism can happen anywhere, its threat is felt everywhere. Because anyone can be its target, everyone feels at risk. Unpredictability magnifies the effect of terrorism's violence and makes it difficult to combat.

The Victims of Terrorism Always Hold Symbolic Value.

The victims of terrorism are not selected purely at random. They are chosen because their identity or location or activities symbolize something the terrorist wants to attack. In 1968, Andreas Baader (co-founder of the German Baader-Meinhof Gang) torched a department store in Frankfurt because it was a symbol of "consumerism." Israeli athletes were attacked at the 1972 Olympic Games in Munich by Palestinians who wanted to strike out at Israel. In 1977, the Red Army Faction (RAF) kidnapped and murdered German industrialist Hans Martin Schleyer because he was seen as a symbol of western capitalism. In 1981, U.S. Army Brigadier General James Dozier was kidnapped by the Red Brigades because he was one of the highest-ranking U.S. military officers stationed in Italy. Also in 1981, Pope John Paul II, for reasons that remain unclear, was targeted for assassination but survived. Unfortunately, Anwar Sadat did not survive a similar attack that year; he was singled out for punishment because he symbolized Arab reconciliation with the state of Israel. In 1984, Prime Minister Margaret Thatcher barely escaped an IRA bombing of the Brighton hotel where

British Conservatives were meeting. Thatcher symbolized the hard-line British approach toward the Irish Republican Army, but specific individuals and heads of state are not the only symbolic targets of terrorist violence. An American airliner, TWA Flight 847, was hijacked in June 1985, beginning an odyssey that took it from Athens to Beirut to Algiers and back to Beirut. The airliner, carrying many Americans (including U.S. Navy Seaman Robert Stethem, who was killed by the hijackers) was chosen because it was an American jet with several American passengers on board. Those Americans held symbolic value to the United States' ally, Israel. In exchange for the release of the hostages, Israel later released over seven hundred Lebanese and Palestinian prisoners being held by the Israeli army. In 1986, Jews worshipping in a Turkish synagogue were the victims of a terrorist attack because of the particular nature of the target. The symbolism of the attack on Turkish Jews was immediately obvious.

The symbolism attached to a terrorist's victim may be personal (Margaret Thatcher and the IRA) or representative (General Dozier of the U.S. Army, industrialist Schleyer, Israeli athletes), or it may be the "everyman" symbolism. Anyone on an American jet or in a Jewish house of worship or sipping expresso at a French café may be singled out as a symbol of the terrorist's choosing. Everyone is potentially vulnerable.

Terrorists Want Publicity.

Terrorist violence is not carried out just to frighten or kill the immediate victims. Terrorism is meant to affect a much wider audience, and to do this terrorism requires publicity. Publicity, propaganda, and psychological warfare—the three P's of terrorism—illustrate why successful terrorism requires news media attention to spread the word about terrorist violence to a larger audience.

Publicity. Terrorist violence has immediate victims, but its real target is a much larger audience. To reach that larger audience, terrorists rely on newspaper, radio, and television reporters and cameramen. The news media and the technology available to spread information around the globe almost instantaneously play an important role in the terrorist strategy. Why does a terrorist want to reach a larger audience? The terrorist wants publicity in order to alter public opinion. Even if the publicity is negative and public opinion is aroused against the terrorist, he believes he is still better off than when he was in an anonymous group with an obscure grievance. Making headline news or receiving prime-time network coverage makes the terrorist important. It draws attention to his cause. Headlines throw the spotlight of public attention on the terrorist. He exploits the news media's desire for a sensational story ("If it bleeds, it leads . . . ") and the public's desire to know about the violence that has been done and perhaps why it was committed.

Propaganda. Once terrorists become the center of public attention, they have the opportunity to promote their cause before a mass audience. This brings many possible benefits to light. Some people will sympathize with the terrorists and support their cause. These newfound supporters may demand that the terrorists be accommodated, putting pressure on the government or the terrorists' enemies to negotiate. Other people will be angered by the terrorist violence and demand that law enforcement officials and government leaders take action to punish the terrorists and prevent future violence. Finally, some people will be frightened by the violence and will be confused by the issues that are involved. These people no longer feel safe in public and often demand greater police protection. All who have witnessed media coverage of terrorism are touched by the violence, and many subsequently make demands on government leaders or other groups to find a way to end the violence. The pressure mounts on government leaders to take action.

Psychological Warfare. When it is most pervasive, the publicity of terrorist violence can become a weapon of psychological warfare. Terrorist groups seeking to destroy or change a government can use well-publicized violence to frighten government officials. (Indira Gandhi of India knew about Sikh death threats; Margaret Thatcher knows that she is still a target of Irish republican assassins who want her to pull British troops out of Northern Ireland.) Terrorist groups also hope that well-publicized violence will convince the public that the government can no longer protect them. Terrorists know that a government crackdown in the wake of terrorism is often unpopular because a crackdown usually includes search and seizure raids, censorship, curfews, interrogations, and arrests. Even if the public doesn't lose total confidence in the state's ability to protect its people, the government nevertheless loses popularity among many people after terrorist violence occurs. The terrorists have managed to wreak damage on the psychological bases of popular support, at very little cost to the terrorists.

Governments, too, use terrorism as a form of psychological warfare against terrorist groups, opponents of the government, and sometimes against the public itself. Such a government uses violence, unpredictably, against its enemies. Some publicity of the violence is necessary so that the news will reach and frighten all the government's opponents. The violent treatment of dissidents by the Soviet Union and Argentina are recent examples of governments that conduct psychological warfare against their opponents by violently intimidating and terrorizing them. Nazi Germany ruled its people by terror, with instruments of psychological warfare that included persecution (of Jews, Communists, homosexuals), midnight arrests, and death camps. Joseph Stalin ruled the Soviet Union by terror for at least five years (1935–1941), sending dissidents and innocents alike to a massive prison camp system (the "Gulag Archipelago"). Anyone could be arrested, all Soviets were vulnerable, and nearly everyone was touched by the terror.

Terrorists Have Political Goals.

Terrorists use violence randomly, and they desire to make an impact beyond their immediate victim. Terrorists also want to make an impact on a wider audience: the witnesses of the violence, the news audience, and often government officials, as well. What kind of impact do terrorists want to make? What sort of goals or objectives are they trying to accomplish? Do they want to do more than just terrify their victims and audience?

Yes, terrorists want to do more than simply "terrify." Terrorists, criminals, and psychopaths all use terror and violence to accomplish their goals. Sometimes their means are similar, but these three groups pursue different objectives. These objectives can be classified as (a) criminal, (b), psychopathological (or insane), and (c) political.

Criminal Terrorism. Criminal behavior involves illegal activity for personal gain. Often a criminal terrorizes his victim in order to reach his goal. The criminal who threatens to burn down a business unless the owner pays "protection" money is terrorizing the victim and other shopkeepers in the area. The loan shark who threatens to kidnap the child of a compulsive gambler unless his betting debts are paid up is using terrorism. Cocaine dealers who assassinate judges, drug enforcement agents, and prosecutors are trying to intimidate and terrorize their opponents in the criminal justice system. (This has happened in Colombia and Mexico, where bribery has also been used to subvert controls on drug trafficking.) Criminal terrorism involves the use of violence and terror strictly for personal gain.

Psychopathic Terror. Although a criminal uses terror for personal gain, a psychopath terrorizes his victims for reasons tied to mental illness and emotional disturbance. When a man climbs to the top of the tallest building on a university campus and begins firing a high-powered rifle at anonymous victims below, insane terrorism has occurred. "Jack the Ripper" of nineteenth-century England terrorized prostitutes in London, serial killers today, such as the "Hillside Strangler," terrorize entire communities for reasons that cannot be made clear to the average person. These acts are violent and unpredictable. The victims sometimes hold symbolic value, and sometimes are chosen purely at random. Publicity's role is not clearly understood in psychoterrorism. What motivates the psychopathological terrorist? What possible benefit can he derive from such actions? Approaching psychoterrorism "logically" does not yield satisfying answers to these questions. Horror for its own sake, a fascination with terror to no particular end other than death: these are the hallmarks of psychopathic terrorism.

Political Terrorism. Most often, when people think of terrorism they focus on political terrorism. Political terrorism is the use of violence or the threat of violence, unpredictable and targeted against symbolic victims, in order to accomplish a political goal. Political goals may include a wide variety of political objectives.

National liberation. Liberation is the stated goal of many organizations and movements that receive publicity following the use of terrorism. The Stern Gang and Irgun (of which former Israeli Prime Minister Menachem Begin was a member) used terrorism to drive the British out of Palestine prior to the establishment of the state of Israel. Today, the Irish Republican Army (IRA) and its provisional wing use terror in Northern Ireland toward a similar end—British withdrawal and the reunification of Ireland. Sikhs from India's Punjab have used terror to publicize their cause and pressure the Indian government to grant autonomy (and ultimately, they hope, independence) to the Sikhs. Many Palestinian groups use terrorism, targeted at Israel or its friends, as a means to express and promote their demand for a Palestinian state. Some groups are committed to the destruction of the state of Israel (as stated in the PLO charter) and replacing it with a Palestinian state. Other groups explain their use of terrorism as the only means available to them for pressuring Israel and its friends to create a Palestinian homeland. The Basque organization ETA (*Euzkadi ta Askatasuna*, or Basque Homeland and Freedom) uses terrorism to promote the creation of a Basque nation state out of three French and four Spanish provinces. These groups and others seeking national liberation are extremely active and responsible for much of the terrorism confronting Europe and the Middle East today.

Political ideology. Many organizations that employ terrorism do not seek to "liberate" their people from occupation or create a new, independent state for them. Instead, some groups use terror in an attempt to alter the political outlook and policies of governments. These groups want to replace the ideology (the beliefs and values) of the state with their own political outlook. Terrorism based on political ideology seeks to alter the fundamental character and behavior of the government. One of the most active ideological movements that uses terrorism is known in the West as Islamic Fundamentalism. Seeking to eradicate Western influence and operate government and society strictly in accordance with Islamic beliefs, members of this movement have been most active in Lebanon. Political terrorism in Lebanon has included bombings (U.S. embassy, Marine barracks compound) to promote U.S. and allied withdrawal, and also skyjackings and kidnappings.

In Europe, political terror has been used by groups that are Marxist or fascist. The *Rote Armee Fraktion* (RAF) or Red Army Faction is the most widely known Marxist organization that uses terrorism in Germany and elsewhere in Europe. This organization (originally known as the Baader-Meinhof Gang) opposes consumerism (1968 attack on a Frankfurt department store), capitalism (1977 abduction and murder of industrialist Hans Martin Schleyer) and military imperalism (numerous attacks on NATO personnel and facilities in the 1980s). It uses terrorism in the hope of sparking revolutionary change in German politics away from liberal, constitutional democracy and toward a Marxist form of government.

There are neo-Nazi and fascist organizations in Europe that also use terrorism to promote their ideas. In Italy, the Marxist Red Brigades have a fascist counterpart, the Black Order. This right-wing group opposes Italy's parliamentary democracy and focuses its use of terrorism against individuals and groups who try to build bridges across Italy's political extremes. Liberal and leftist newspapers and offices have been bombed by fascist groups, but their most recent headlines have come from the Bologna train station bombing.

In the United States, political-ideologial terrorism occurred during the Vietnam war protests and again in the mid-1980s with a new target: abortion clinics. Groups that had failed to alter abortion laws turned to more violent methods of attracting publicity to their cause and pressuring government officials. The violence has been unpredictable and symbolic. The objective continues to be bringing an end to the belief that abortion should be legal and to halt abortion on demand. The FBI, however, does not classify these bombings as acts of terrorism.

The political motivations of terrorism, either national liberation or ideological, set political terrorism apart from criminal or psychopathic terrorism. Reasonable people can and do disagree whether political motivations justify violence, and political terrorists usually exploit the same weapons of terror that criminals and psychopaths use against their victims. The political goals of groups using terrorism, however, are a useful and necessary component of defining terrorism and understanding why it takes place.

Terrorism Has Great Flexibility.

One of the unique features of terrorism is its flexibility. Anyone can use it—governments, groups, or individuals; anyone can be its target—governments (Israel), organizations (NATO), groups (Soviet dissidents), individuals (Pope John Paul II, Anwar al-Sadat), or anonymous victims in the wrong place at the wrong time. Unlike wars—which only states or large, well-armed movements can conduct—terrorism can be a small-group, inexpensive operation. Interstate wars are usually confined to a geographical area and a declared set of combatants, whereas terrorism can be conducted widely, across many national borders with relative ease. The harm terrorists actually inflict is small, seemingly out of proportion to the fear they generate by their use of symbolism and media coverage. In peacetime, there are no armies to deter the threat of violence that terrorists pose, and there are no rules to limit terrorism as rules of war are meant to restrict the behavior of armies. The flexibility of terrorism is visible in its evolution from an "internal" problem (that governments could repress) to an "international" problem that states and the community of states in the United Nations cannot eliminate.

"International" terrorism crosses national boundaries by choosing a foreign target, committing a terrorist act abroad, or trying to influence the behavior of a foreign group or government. Terrorism within a state may become an international issue, as well, as in the case of private American assistance to Irish nationalist groups, or the World Psychiatric Association's criticism of Soviet abuses of psychiatry in terrorizing dissidents.

Terrorism is an Issue of Great Complexity.

Terrorism is a complex issue that involves many forms of violence, many different motivations, and no proven solutions. Terrorism has many faces and many components. It challenges the police, courts, intelligence agencies, national governments, and the United Nations. Terrorism also involves business, the media, and diplomats, but no single group alone can deal successfully with it. It is a powerful concept, and people who can agree on a general definition often cannot agree on when to apply it. There is widespread agreement on these elements of terrorism:

> Terrorism is unpredictable violence or the threat of violence. It targets symbolic victims and exploits publicity to obtain political goals through coercion. It can be used by groups or states against groups or states.

The complexity of terrorism also lies in disagreements over when to employ it as a label. Individuals and governments often use many or all of these elements to describe or define terrorism. If they approve of a particular terrorist's political goals, however, they will reject the label of terrorism to describe the terrorist's behavior. At that point, the terrorist is called a "freedom fighter," *"mujahedeen,"* or "soldier in the struggle for national liberation." States that use terrorism to govern or as an instrument of foreign policy enjoy "plausible deniability" and can refuse to acknowledge their participation in terrorism. The complexity of terrorism is further increased by the implicit negative value judgment that accompanies the concept and by the debates revolving around its application. In this book, the concept will be applied to behavior that includes the components listed above.

Why Study Terrorism?

Aside from the publicity surrounding terrorism, these are several important reasons why it deserves our careful attention.

Terrorism Affects Us Individually.

Perhaps the most frightening aspect of terrorism is that it can strike anyone, anywhere. Where it occurs often, individuals change their behavior. Children grow up in Ulster with emotional problems. Religious pilgrims avoid visiting the Holy Land. Family vacations to Europe are canceled. Friends and relatives share the grief of mourning deaths like the ones suffered by Leon Klinghoffer, who died in the *Achille Lauro* hijacking, and Robert Dean Stethem, who was killed in the TWA 847 hijacking.

Terrorism Is a Product of Our High Technology
Culture and Has Affected Modern Culture in Ways We
Have Only Begun to Assess.

The mobility of terrorists, the destructiveness of their attacks, and the global publicity they can obtain reveal how well terrorists have exploited modern technology. The advances in communications, transportation, and weaponry that are the hallmarks of the twentieth century have been turned to purposes we never anticipated.

American culture has begun to accommodate terrorism, too. "Nightline" was an evening news program designed originally to update Americans on the Tehran hostage crisis involving U.S. diplomats (1979– 1981); it is now a fixture on late-night network television. Americans walk through metal detectors at airports without complaints and queue up patiently to have their carry-on luggage x-rayed. Local police, the FBI, and the Pentagon all have teams trained and ready to handle terrorist/hostage situations. Journalists everywhere know the public is interested in terrorism. In 1986, "NBC News" broadcast an interview with Palestinian terrorist Abu Abbas during the prime-time news hours, while tourists in Washington, D.C., no longer seem to notice the barricades set up to block truck bombs from striking the State Department building or the White House.

Terrorism Affects Our Foreign Policy.

Terrorism can influence the course of a nation's foreign policy. The diplomats who carry out U.S. foreign policy and the U.S. embassies where they work have become targets of terrorism. The 1983 bombing of the U.S. embassy in Beirut and, later that same year, the truck-bomb attack on the Marine barracks compound helped force an American withdrawal from Lebanon. The U.S. State Department confronts new problems created by terrorism. For example, is it legal (under international law) to bomb Libya after U.S. servicemen in Berlin are killed in a bombing that might have been ordered by Libyan leader Kaddafi? Is it diplomatically wise to force a jet carrying suspected terrorists to land on Italian soil? How can a suspected terrorist be extradited from Germany when German citizens are being held hostage to prevent such an extradition to the United States? Should the United States negotiate with terrorists holding U.S. citizens hostage?

Terrorism has focused U.S. foreign policy on a new set of problems and actors. Terrorism has also created new strains in alliances and relationships that the United States considers very important. The issue of aid to the Nicaraguan "contras" became involved in negotiations with Iran to release Americans held hostage in Beirut. U.S.-German relations were strained by problems in the extradition of a suspect in the hijacking of TWA Flight 847 in June 1985 to Beirut. The U.S. ambassadors to the United Nations have labored long and hard and unsuccessfully to coordinate an international effort to put an end to terrorism. Terrorism continues to absorb more energy and demand more attention from the foreign policy bureaucracy (in diplomacy, military, and intelligence agencies). Terrorism has complicated many friendly relationships and created a new source of contention in the United Nations. Terrorism has also added to U.S.-Soviet tensions as Soviet aid to some terrorist organizations is made public. The ramifications of terrorism in U.S. foreign policy must be studied. It is a new and serious challenge to American efforts to promote national interests at home and abroad.

Terrorism Is the Newest Fixture in International Relations.

Terrorism is the latest addition to the repertoire of techniques that states use to interact with each other. Terrorism is involved in the process of state construction (Israel) and destruction (Lebanon, Northern Ireland), and it also represents a new way in which the superpowers now compete. In the nuclear age, "less is more," and the United States and Soviet Union have found that it is often safer to compete by sponsoring proxies or by backing terrorist groups. The United States backs Afghanistan's *mujahedeen*, "freedom fighters" who also use terror tactics against the Soviet troops occupying their country. The Soviets funnel aid to Palestinian groups trying to destroy Israel, an important U.S. ally. Soviet allies, Libya and Syria, have aided European organizations (Red Army Faction) that oppose and attack U.S. troops stationed at NATO bases. In the nuclear age, sponsoring terrorist groups is less costly and runs a lower risk of a superpower confrontation that possibly might escalate to a nuclear exchange.

In the Middle East, many governments (including Iran, Iraq, Libya, and Syria) provide assistance and sanctuary to organizations that use terrorism to achieve their goals. The United States withdrew its troops from Lebanon a few months after the devastating truck bomb attack on the Marine compound in Beirut (October 1983), an attack that U.S. intelligence reports had support from outside Lebanon. Middle Eastern states sponsor terrorist groups to subvert other governments, including Lebanon, Israel, and many Arab states, as well. In this area, terrorism appears to have replaced warfare as the preferred mode of interstate conflict.

Terrorism is the new phenomenon of international relations, not because it is new (which it is not) but because many states now use it to exert influence on other states, and because terrorism plays a very visible role in the creation and dismantling of states and governments.

Terrorism Touches on Many of the Ethical Questions That Arise in the Study of Politics.

Terrorism raises some of the perennial questions in international politics, especially the question of "When is violence justifiable?" Terrorism is often employed in struggles for national liberation or national self-determination. One must ask, "How many lives is national independence worth?" Terrorism involves weighing the value of human life against the importance of certain political causes, including the cause of freedom. When terrorism appears, however, freedom from fear disappears. Living in fear makes the targets of terrorism willing to pay a high price to regain their sense of security. Sometimes the price is very high, indeed.

Terrorism brings together the struggle for power and freedom, the taking of innocent life alongside heroic self-sacrifice. Terrorism involves the clash of "rights" and the zealotry of fanatics. At some point, citizens and leaders must decide where they stand on the ethical dilemmas terrorism creates. There will be no security in remaining ignorant.

Organization of the Text

In the following chapters the complex nature of terrorism is examined through a series of illustrations and contrasting examples. In chapter 2, the history of terrorism as an old and ubiquitous phenomenon is explored, beginning with the Jewish Zealots (A.D. 6–135). The use of state terror in the French revolution and the role of terrorism in nineteenth-century anarchist thought are discussed to establish the historical flexibility of terrorism, both as an instrument of governance and as a revolutionary device.

Chapter 3 considers one of the primary sources of terrorism: old and frustrated struggles for national liberation. Five cases (Irish, Armenian, Palestinian, Sikh, and Basque) are presented to illustrate the common thread running through much modern terrorism.

In contrast to nationalistic terrorism, chapter 4 discusses how states govern through terror. Two modern examples—one from the right (the Argentine "Dirty War") and one from the left (the Soviet use of psychiatric terror)—are used to illustrate the flexibility and the high tech nature of modern state terrorism.

Chapter 5 examines radical ideologies as a source of terrorism. Three illustrations are used to demonstrate religious (Islamic), right-wing (Ku Klux Klan), and left-wing (Red Army Faction) types of belief systems that call for terrorism to promote political goals.

In chapter 6, the role of media competition and coverage of modern terrorism are discussed in the context of liberal democracies that are targets of terrorism. British, West German, and U.S. media response to terrorism are compared and contrasted.

Chapter 7 considers terrorism as a tool of foreign policy, especially for the superpowers in the age of avoiding nuclear war while competing around the globe.

Chapter 8 focuses on the response of four liberal democracies (United Kingdom, Federal Republic of Germany, Israel, and the United States) to illustrate the different pitfalls that confront states that want national security *and* civil liberties.

Chapter 9 considers why international law and the United Nations have failed to control or punish terrorism and also looks at interstate efforts that have succeeded.

Summary

Defining terrorism is a controversial exercise, but the numerous definitions of terrorism frequently share certain common elements. These include

The use or threat of violence,

Unpredictability or randomness,

A symbolic target,

Publicity, and

Political goals.

Terrorism is essentially and inescapably a political concept, and most debates actually hinge on whether or not to describe certain activities as terrorist. Terrorism is not an instrument solely of the weak; terrorism has often been used by states to govern, and it has become an increasingly common instrument of foreign policy, as well.

The flexibility of terrorism has made it a unique fixture in modern international relations. Because terrorism exploits modern technology (of communications, travel, and weaponry); because it plays a role in the construction and destruction of states; and because it has become a foreign policy option for governments (particularly the Superpowers), we must study terrorism as one of the essential components of international relations.

Finally, terrorism encompasses many of the recurring problems of political ethics: How can democracies preserve civil liberties when confronted by the threat of terrorism? When is violence justified? How is violence justified by those using it? Terrorism is a complex and pervasive problem in international politics. It is an old phenomenon that has been invested with a lethal new energy and now threatens an increasingly interdependent world.

2
Terrorism Past

Terrorism has an old pedigree; its roots can be traced back to societies that developed in what we think of as the cradle of civilization. Greek philosophers and Roman historians studied what today we call terrorism. The leading philosophers of ancient Greece, Socrates and Aristotle, gave us the idea of *tyrannicide*, the justifiable assassination of a ruler who governs capriciously or debases or abuses his people. Flavius Josephus, a Roman historian who was also a Jew, wrote a detailed account of one of the earliest, systematic terrorist campaigns. That campaign of Jewish zealots against the Romans in Palestine (A.D. 6–135) is the first of three historical terrorist campaigns this chapter will examine. After reviewing the Zealots and their use of political terrorism, this chapter will then consider state terrorism in the eighteenth century in the course of the French Revolution and anarchist terrorism in the nineteenth century as a prelude to the Russian revolutions.

They have a passion for liberty that is almost inconquerable.[1]

The Zealots' Campaign of Terror against Roman Rule

Jewish patriots who opposed Roman rule in Palestine called themselves *zealots*, meaning they were "zealous" for God and "zealous" in their attempts to establish national independence. The Zealots first appeared in Jewish history in A.D. 6 when Rome ordered a census for the purpose of tax collections. (This was the same census mentioned in the New Testament, which coincided with the birth of Jesus.) The Zealots fought Roman rule in numerous ways, including assassinations and guerrilla attacks on Roman personnel and installations. The Zealots sparked an uprising in A.D. 6, which the Roman army crushed and ended by crucifying two thousand

Zealots. (Crucifixion was a form of execution reserved for thieves and rebels.) The Zealots succeeded, however, in establishing a political philosophy that linked religious and political beliefs into a call for action against the Roman occupation. Those religious and political motivations would persist until Rome destroyed the Jews' temple (A.D. 70) and dispersed them from Palestine (135 A.D.).

Early Jewish terrorism against Roman occupation fulfilled all the criteria of terrorism described in chapter 1. Zealots used violence (assassination, hit-and-run attacks) against Romans as well as Greeks and Jews who sympathized or collaborated with Roman rule. The attacks were unpredictable and the targets held symbolic value; victims were Roman officials or high-ranking Jews who were profiting from Roman rule. The attacks often took place publicly or on a holy day, so that word of the Zealots' attack would spread as quickly as possible and as widely as possible. The Zealots' goals were political: they wanted to end Roman rule and create a state in which the only authority over people would be God. Roman law would be replaced by the Torah, and God would be the sole lord of the land. The early Zealots were often described as fanatics with a passion for liberty and contempt for death, and this reputation heightened the fear their attacks produced.

After the Romans suppressed the first wave of terrorism, the Jewish nationalists were quiet for nearly half a century. In the middle of the first century A.D., terrorists became active in Jewish cities. Again, the targets were Romans or Jews who collaborated with the Roman occupation. Terrorists of this period were known as *sicarii*, or "men of the dagger," and they killed their victims with a *sica* or a small dagger. The *sicarii* often operated in large crowds, killing their targets at close range and then disappearing into the crowd before the deed was discovered. The public relations impact of such a murder was quite powerful. Every person in the crowd was vulnerable, and Romans and prominent collaborators felt threatened whenever they mingled with the public. The act was difficult to prevent, and the *sicarii* were difficult to capture. When Flavius Josephus wrote of the *sicarii* and Zealots, he referred to them as criminals, bandits, brigands, and looters, among other derogatory labels. There certainly were criminals in Palestine during this time, but the *sicarii* were not robbing their victims or extorting protection money. The targets were not chosen on a psychopath's whim, but were selected for their political symbolic value, and the public knew this. Although Flavius Josephus and Roman authorities labeled the *sicarii* criminals and ignored their political motivations, the public generally understood that *sicarii* violence was rooted in a bitter determination to reject any ruler but God.

The culmination of anti-Roman terrorism began in A.D. 66 when Zealot groups (they were never organized into a tightly disciplined organization) massacred a Roman garrison and occupied the temple in Jerusalem. This triggered the Roman-Jewish War (A.D. 66–70) that ended when Titus destroyed the Jews' temple (A.D. 70) and Silva besieged and took the fortress of Masada (A.D. 73–74). The intertwining of religious and political beliefs with the use of violence and terror makes this one of the most fascinating episodes of terrorism's long history.

The Zealots believed that they were called by God to fight a Holy War against the force of darkness, i.e., Roman rule over the Jews. The Zealots believed that such a war was inevitable if they were obedient to God's command to respect no ruler over Israel except God alone. To do this required that they refuse to submit to Roman authority and trust, as Flavius Josephus wrote, that "Heaven would be their zealous helper" (*Antiquities* 18:23). But the Zealots did not believe in passive resistance. The Zealots were ancient practitioners of the belief "God helps those who help themselves" and trusted that if their obedience to God provoked a war, then God would intervene and deliver them from the Romans. Never expecting to defeat Rome outright, the Zealots challenged the Romans and then played a major role in the ensuing war.

After early Zealot victories, the Romans regrouped and laid siege to Jerusalem, occupied by several Zealot sects. Some historians believe that the Zealots sealed their fate there when they switched from terrorist tactics and guerrilla warfare[2] to confront the Roman army in traditional combat. When Jerusalem fell (A.D. 70), the Zealots fled to fortress sanctuaries in the countryside. There they lost the mobility and anonymity that had made their terrorist violence so threatening. The Romans followed them and besieged the fortresses until they fell, one by one. Eventually, only one Zealot stronghold was left—Masada.

At Masada the patriotism and fanaticism of Zealot terrorism reached its pinnacle, although in the end the violence was directed by the Zealots against themselves. Holed up in their fortress south of Jerusalem, the Zealots continued to conduct terrorist attacks from Masada until the Romans encircled and sealed off the mountain stronghold. While the Romans brought in seige machines, the Zealots waited for a saving miracle. Their religious and nationalistic zeal had brought them from anonymous attacks on Romans to a confrontation with the military prowess of imperial Rome. Historian Flavius Josephus, who was at Masada, recounted the speech given by Eleazar, the Zealots' leader, the day before the Romans entered the fortress:

> Let us spare nothing but our provisions. They will be a testimonial when we are dead that we were not subdued for want of the basic necessities, but that according to our original resolution, we have preferred death before slavery.[3]

Even in death, Eleazar anticipated the impact of violence on the Romans. The Zealots committed mass suicide: 960 men, women, and children died by their own hand. When the Romans entered Masada the next day, they found the bodies and the food supply intact, and only a half-dozen survivors, who had hidden themselves and lived to report the mass suicide.

Masada was silent testimony to the depth of the Zealots' religious and political commitment. In the end, they used the last and only form of resistance left them: suicidal violence. Flavius Josephus recorded the Roman reaction when they took Masada:

> They met with the multitude of the slain, but could take no pleasure in the fact, though it were done to their enemies. Nor could they do other than wonder at the courage of their resolution, and the immovable contempt of death which so great a number of them had shown.[4]

After Masada, the Romans tracked down and executed Zealots who had fled to Egypt, but terrorism continued sporadically in Palestine. The political goals of the Zealots and the religious beliefs in which those goals were rooted did not die easily. More terrorism and two more rebellions (A.D. 116–117 and A.D. 132–135) took place before the Romans took the drastic measure of expelling Jews from their homeland. To put an end to Jewish terrorism and rebellion, the Roman Empire had to scatter the Jews.

The scattering, however, did not destroy the Jews' strong sense of nationalism and religious motivation. Those strong convictions helped Jews maintain their identity through their wanderings, until a Jewish state providing a refuge for Jews and respecting their faith was established in 1948. Recreating the Jewish state also involved violence and terrorism on the part of both Arabs and Jews. Eighteen centuries later, the history of terrorism had come full cycle. From the early violence against Romans in the time of Christ, to the expulsion of Jews from their homeland, to the return to Israel, terrorism played a key role in the political processes that destroyed and rebuilt the Jewish state. Those processes are still at work in the region today. (See chapter 3, on the Palestinians.)

Terror in the French Revolution

A French governmental decree on September 5, 1793 declared, "Terror is the order of the day." Terrorism has been used both to destroy and build states, making terrorism a highly flexible tool for political change. Terrorism did not play a significant role in the early phases of the French Revolution when the nobles (1787–1788) rejected the bankrupt rule of King Louis XVI or when a liberal revolution (1789–1791) that included moderate and middle-class elements took control of the state. Terrorism appeared in the third phase (1792–1794) of the revolution, the "popular" phase when prisons were stormed and inmates were massacred by mobs hunting for those behind the hardships (food shortages, inflation) that France was enduring. The Terror, as it is known, originated in chaos with the September Massacres of 1792, but the Great Terror was organized by the government and set into motion the following year (1793). The Great Terror was systematic and deliberate; it was an organized, ruthless policy that the state used to attack its many problems. The Reign of Terror (September 1793– July 1794) is one of the earliest cases of state terrorism wherein we can study a government intentionally and systematically using terrorism to achieve political goals.

> Anarchy within, invasion from without. A country cracking from outside pressure, disintegrating from internal strain. Revolution at its height. War. Inflation. Hunger. Fear. Hate. Sabotage.[5]

Three questions arise in studying the Great Terror: (1) Under what circumstances did the French government choose a policy of terrorism? (2) How did the government carry out that policy? (3) What effect did the Great Terror have? Many experts believe that crisis conditions forced the French government to use terrorism to defend the country and preserve the revolution from internal and external threats. France was at war with England, Holland, Prussia, Austria, Spain, Portugal, Sicily, Sardinia, and Piedmont. French ports were blockaded; there was great concern over desertions from the army; and there was fear of military plots to reverse the revolution. The cost of the foreign wars and the blockade of French ports had added to the economic crisis that gripped France. Poor harvests and food shortages, hoarders and commodity speculators had caused hunger and discontent across the country. Not only was there great pressure on the government to improve popular living conditions, but several factions were at work trying to alter the course of the revolution. Opponents of the revolution who had fled the country, especially emigré nobles, conspired with belligerent nations (especially England) to make a counterrevolution. Royalist sympathizers, some of the clergy (the revolution was hostile to the Roman Catholic Church), and federalists who opposed a dominant central government sparked various uprisings in the west and southeast, including Bordeaux, Caen, Toulon, Lyon, Marseilles, and the Vendée. These revolts threatened to splinter France and terminate the revolution. The government was confronted by not one but many crises: the threat of foreign invasion and civil war, economic hardship, and counterrevolution. By the autumn of 1793, the government faced the possibility of a complete breakdown in state authority, i.e., anarchy. Its response was the Great Terror, or in the words of Hippolyte Carnot, a member of the government, "the Terror was a dictatorship of distress."

The great curiosity of this crisis was not that the government fought for its survival and the survival of the revolution, but how systematically and bureaucratically the government's response took shape. The machinery and legislation that made the Great Terror possible were created for the most part in 1793; those institutions that predated the Terror were consolidated to serve the government's policy. The most important cog in the machinery of the Great Terror was the Committee on Public Safety, established by the government in April 1793. The committee's size hovered around a dozen, and its leading member, citizen Robespierre, joined it in July. The Revolutionary Tribunal investigated, arrested, tried, and executed "enemies of the revolution," aided in the countryside by Watch Committees and Deputies on Mission. The Committee of General Security and the revolutionary army (separate from the national army) comprised the remainder of the terror machinery, but the brains behind the official terror was the Committee on Public Safety. The bureaucratic machinery created by the government was assisted by legislation passed in the fall of 1793; foremost among the new legislation was the "Law of Suspected Persons" passed on September 17, 1793.

The Law of Suspects, as it has become known, authorized the arrest of all "suspected persons" still at liberty in France. This legislation marked the government's declaration of war on its internal enemies. Aristocrats, clergy, and emigrés not loyal to the new government, as well as federalists and profiteers—all were targeted by the Law of Suspects for arrest and speedy prosecution. The government, through the Committee on Public Safety, set out to punish, destroy, or intimidate its enemies. Taking its cue from this legislation, the Revolutionary Tribunals began ordering the execution of prisoners long since in state custody, beginning with the former queen of France, Marie Antoinette, who went to the guillotine October 16, 1793. (King Louis XVI had been beheaded on January 21 of that same year.) The terrorism directed against suspected enemies of the revolution included arrest, imprisonment, confiscation of property, and execution. (The guillotine had been developed as a more "humane," sure, and swift method of execution, although some died in the Terror by hanging, shooting, or drowning.) The Terror consisted of arrests, executions, and—most important—the fear of arrest and execution. The bureaucratically minded Committee and Tribunal kept records of their work, and statistical studies show that between one hundred thousand and three hundred thousand suspects were detained in the Reign of Terror[6] and that thirty-five thousand to forty thousand deaths[7] resulted directly from arrests made at the time. (Approximately 16,600 death sentences[8] were issued, but many more individuals died in inadequate, overcrowded prisons.)

The goal of the Committee on Public Safety was to punish the enemies of revolutionary France and to intimidate those it could not reach. Political enemies were the primary targets of the Terror (although economic crimes were also of concern), and on October 10, 1793, the government suspended the Constitution of 1793 and declared that the government would be "revolutionary" until peace arrived. Effectively this meant France had an emergency or war government that was headed by the Committee on Public Safety. The revolutionary government also claimed "the right to use terror against its enemies."[9] Robespierre believed the government owed its enemies nothing except death.

The Committee on Public Safety and the Revolutionary Tribunals (quadrupled in size to handle the Terror) centralized control of the terror (although a significant amount of unofficial terror took place in the countryside). From March through September 1793, 518 death sentences[10] were carried out; from October 1793 to May 1794, 10,812 death sentences[11] were handed down; and, from June to July 1794, 2,554 death sentence[12] were carried out. The height of the Reign of Terror saw prisoners waiting on line behind the guillotine and large crowds gathered to witness the executions. Sensational publicity accompanied the execution of the state's enemies, further spreading the Terror and the fear it was meant to instill.

The government continued to concentrate authority in the hands of the Committee to fight the chaos that threatened to consume France and the revolution. The "Constitution of the Terror," as it has been called, was approved on December 4, 1793, and it enabled the Committee to continue its policy of state terror to rid France of its "enemies." The agencies of the Terror, having begun the consolidation of state power and the destruction of traitors and enemies, turned next to the last political goal of the Terror: ideological reform. Robespierre, through the Committee, set out to mold France into a Republic of Virtue, based on Rousseau's model of a utopian society. He wrote:

> The aim of popular government in a time of revolution is virtue and terror
> at one and the same time: virtue without which terror is disastrous, terror
> without which virtue is impotent.[13]

By the middle of the winter of 1794, the French government had crushed the rebel revolt in the Vendée and evicted the English from their occupation of Toulon. Success appeared likely in both the foreign and civil wars, and there was growing concern over the Committee's experiment with Terror to consolidate state authority and defeat internal and external foes. Another effect of the Terror soon became evident: it had proven so useful and effective that some members of the Committee wanted to continue the Reign of Terror. Robespierre, among others, held a political vision of an ideal French republic based on Rousseau's idea of virtue and the "general will." Robespierre "was a revolutionist who, having an ideal commonwealth in view, saw in the execution of its possible enemies the only method by which it could be established."[14] When the general public lost touch with Robespierre's vision, he used propaganda campaigns, cooptation, and repression to direct or stifle public criticism of his vision. When other revolutionaries called for an end to the Terror and the return to constitutional government, Robespierre turned the Terror against his critics. For Robespierre, the goal of democratic perfection justified the use of terrorism; he had become "terror personified."[15]

Robespierre's leading critic, Danton, had supported the Reign of Terror when it seemed the only means for preserving France. By spring 1794, Danton opposed the continued use of state terrorism, and for his opposition to the Committee's policy he was arrested, condemned, and executed. The Reign of Terror, initiated to defend the state and reestablish order, quickly became unpopular as the Committee used terrorism to eliminate its ideological opponents. In May 1794, attempts were made to assassinate Robespierre. By July, the Terror had become so unpopular that Robespierre himself was arrested and executed. Most of the machinery of the Terror was eliminated within a year.

Why did the Reign of Terror end so abruptly and what were its effects? Two explanations, not exclusive of one another, are usually cited to explain the rapid decline of state terror. The Terror was popularly supported and justified when the danger to the state and the revolution was greatest. When those dangers were eliminated by the army's success in war and the Committee's success in eliminating enemies at home, popular support for the Terror dropped off quickly. In addition to success, the Terror was brought to a close by the government when members of the government themselves began falling victim to the machinery of the Terror. Once it became clear that Robespierre believed he could use terrorism without popular or broad governmental support, the terrorism had to end. In September 1794, the Committee of General Security regained control of the police from the Committee on Public Safety. In May 1795, the Revolutionary Tribunal was put out of commission, and on October 28, 1795, the Executive Directory was established to rule France.

The effects of the Reign of Terror were many and varied. State terror helped quell dissent within France by destroying or intimidating the revolution's opponents. The Reign of Terror helped preserve the state and the revolution and also contributed to centralizing power in the capital. The repression and terror used by the Committee on Public Safety proved difficult to control and became unpopular once the crises threatening France diminished. When the Reign of Terror ended, there was a brutal reaction known as the "White Terror" (September 1794–September 1795) in which government agents suspected of participating in the Great Terror were hunted down by mobs and put to death. The Great Terror, born in the anarchy of massacres and civil war in 1792, gave birth to another year of anarchy and terror when it ended with Robespierre's execution. The government that replaced the Revolutionary Government was much more conservative than Robespierre and the Jacobins, and ruled with repression and the assistance of the military. R. R. Palmer claims that the Terror represented the transition from anarchy to dictatorship in France,[16] and the conservative constitutional government soon gave way to the rule of Napoleon and the army. Others who have studied the revolution and the terrorism it generated believe that Robespierre and the Committee blazed a new path toward mass tyranny,[17] for they governed not with the power of police or armies, but with the weapon of mass terror.

The state terrorism used in revolutionary France was an ugly yet fascinating development in the history of terrorism. Its usefulness in consolidating state power, destroying enemies, and intimidating opposition was firmly established. Terror had become an instrument of state construction as well as destruction.

The Russian Anarchists and "Propaganda by the Deed"

Terrorism is as flexible as it is old. Zealots used terrorism (A.D. 6–135) trying to liberate the Holy Land and Jews from Roman rule; the revolutionary government in France used the Reign of Terror (1792–1794) to intimidate and eliminate its enemies. To understand modern terrorism with its blending of ideology and nationalistic fervor, it is useful to consider the rationale and terror tactics of anarchists in the nineteenth century. Anarchist philosophy and terrorist activity in Europe during the latter half of the nineteenth century, especially the work of Russian anarchists, hold important keys for understanding much of today's antistate terrorism.

> Anarchy is a horrible calamity, but it is less horrible than despotism. Where anarchy has slain its hundreds, despotism has sacrificed millions upon millions. . . . Anarchy is short-lived mischief, while despotism is all but immortal.[18]

William Godwin (1756–1836), an Englishman, and Pierre Proudhon (1809–1865), a Frenchman, often are called the fathers of anarchism. Their ideas profoundly affected many young Europeans, especially Russian expatriates who wanted to change the status quo in Europe. Godwin believed that modern institutions (powerful government, fixed laws, and private property) corrupted human society. Proudhon took these ideas further in his writing, considered by many to be radical and provocative. Proudhon called his philosophy "an-archie," meaning "no-government," and he rejected the ideas of the state, laws, and private property. It was Proudhon who claimed "property is theft,"[19] but more important he also rejected all government-made laws. "I will have no laws; I acknowledge none; I protest against every order which an ostensibly necessary authority shall please to impose on my free will."[20] Proudhon believed that whenever one person governed another, slavery appeared, and that social relations instead should be based on contracts freely entered into and respected. He believed his ideas could be popularized and people could be persuaded to abolish laws, private property, and the state; but Proudhon also believed that violence was inherent in human nature, what he called the tendency to destroy and build again (*destruam et aedificabo*). The ideas of Godwin and Proudhon were circulating in Western Europe when young Russian expatriates and exiles began to arrive. They would contribute Russian elements to anarchist philosophy and spark outbursts of terrorist violence that would rock Europe for decades.

Mikhail Bakunin (1814–1876) left a career in the Russian Imperial Guard to study in Germany and France. There he encountered Proudhon's anarchist philosophy and became active in groups promoting revolutions in Russia, Poland, and Germany. In his political writing and agitation, Bakunin drew together the strands of anarchist philosophy and the Russian tradition of violent outbursts against authority. He wove those strands into a movement that would challenge Karl Marx's control of the socialist International and laid the groundwork for political terrorism that would become known as "propaganda by the deed."

Bakunin adopted the anarchist call for an end to the state, laws, and private property. Unlike Proudhon, who believed people could be convinced to abolish those institutions, Bakunin argued that the "old order" would have to be overthrown by a violent social revolution. Bakunin spoke of himself as a revolutionist who used action and deeds, not philosophy, to change the system. Bakunin believed that social change could be made to come about quickly and that initial acts of violence were necessary to show people the way to overturn the old order. For Bakunin, the destructiveness of violence was necessary and useful. "The urge of destruction is at the same time a creative urge!" he declared in his first article in 1842, in which Bakunin called for "destruction—terrible, total, inexorable and universal"[21] to eliminate all repressive governments. For Bakunin, violence was useful in showing that the police state was not omnipotent. Violent acts could reveal natural human virtues as it swept away depraved institutions. Bakunin's call for violence eventually led to his deportation to and imprisonment in Russia. The tsar exiled Bakunin to Siberia, from which he escaped and made his way back to Europe by way of America.

Once back in Europe, Bakunin resumed writing and working with anarchist, communist, and socialist groups. He continued to oppose all organized authority, but when his path crossed that of his fellow countryman and expatriate, Sergei Nechaev, violent Russian anarchism began to evolve into a modern form of terrorism. Nechaev and Bakunin met in Switzerland, and there the old and young expatriates wrote the *Revolutionary Catechism*; this "guide" to revolutionaries said that ruthless terror was necessary in the fight to destroy the state. Nechaev himself called for personal, violent, and immediate action, and soon Bakunin agreed that terrorism was the most effective means to undermine the values and control of the state. The *Catechism* put the revolutionist/terrorist outside the bounds of the law and called for victory at any price. The revolutionist, it said, "has broken every connection with the social order. Should he continue to live in it, it will be solely for the purpose of destroying it the more surely. . . . To him, whatever aids the triumph of the cause is ethical; all that which hinders it is unethical."[22] In the collaboration with Nechaev, Bakunin also elaborated on the "secret societies" he thought were necessary to make a revolution happen, to organize and speed the process of violent and rapid social upheaval. Bakunin's experiences in Russia, including his fear of secret police and informers, led to his fascination with secret organizations. Working with Nechaev, Bakunin set up several secret organizations (International Brotherhood, Secret Alliance) that were similar in character to many modern terrorist organizations today. Nechaev "proclaimed and acted on the hypothesis that morality does not exist,"[23] and the use of ruthless violence was popularized through articles and pamphlets. Soon after the *Revolutionary Catechism* was written, Bakunin and Nechaev had a falling out. Nechaev was arrested and deported back to Russia, where he died in the tsar's prison. The work of honing anarchist philosophy into an instrument of terror and propaganda fell to another Russian expatriate, Prince Peter Kropotkin.

> A single deed makes more propaganda in a few days than a thousand pamphlets. The government rages pitilessly; but by this it only causes further deeds to be committed and drives the insurgents to heroism. One deed brings forth another; opponents join the meeting; the government splits into factions; harshness intensifies the conflict; concessions come too late; the revolution breaks out.[24]

Peter Kropotkin (1842–1921), a member of an old, noble Russian family, had fled to Europe after escaping from the tsar's prison in 1876. He had been converted to anarchism during an earlier visit to Switzerland and was circulating anarchist propaganda in Russian when the secret police arrested him. In exile, Kropotkin wrote extensively, laying down the arguments justifying terrorism and "permanent revolt by word of mouth, in writing, by the dagger, the gun, dynamite. . . . Everything which is illegal is acceptable to us."[25]

Peter Kropotkin opposed the reformist ideas of Proudhon. Kropotkin believed that terrorism was one of the few tools available to the people to resist government and trigger a mass revolt. Progressive ideas had to be brought to life through action, not just propaganda, and Kropotkin was convinced that the first acts of the revolution would be destructive. "Law is valueless and harmful,"[26] he wrote, "How much trash there is to clear away!"[27] Kropotkin's contemporary, Paul Brousse, coined the phrase "propaganda by the deed" in 1877 to capture the notion of using terror to awaken the public's conscience. Kropotkin agreed that propaganda by the word had only limited impact and must be complemented with propaganda by the deed. He believed that acts of political violence—i.e., terrorism— could transform popular dissent into a social revolution. Soon the idea of individual acts of terrorism spread across Europe. In Austria-Hungary, Belgium, France, Germany, Italy, Spain, and Switzerland the idea of using anarchist violence and propaganda by the deed to trigger revolutionary change gained popularity and practitioners. Individual terrorists would need very little in the way of financing and organization as they created wave after wave of violence hoping to trigger revolutions throughout Europe.

> Il n'y a pas d'innocents.
> (There are no innocent victims.)[28]

Inspired by the ideas of Bakunin, Nechaev, and Kropotkin, terrorists began to wreak destruction that was terrible and inexorable across the continent. (The reputation of the anarchists would become so fierce and notorious that they found themselves banned from entering the United States altogether.) In western Europe, terrorist attacks were symbolic and highly ideological; violence was the "supreme posture of defiance, the retribution for the sins of capitalism"[29] and state government. The wave of terrorism began in 1878 in Italy with an attempt on the life of King Umberto, for many anarchists believed that oppression could be ended by murdering the oppressors.[30] This attempt was followed by attacks on Umberto's wife, the German Emperor, Spanish King Alfonso XII, Tsar Alexander II, the Empress of Austria, U.S. President McKinley, and French President Carnot.

The terrorists did not limit themselves to assassination; bombings were also a spectacular success in generating publicity or "propaganda by the deed." Anarchists were particularly busy in France, beginning in 1881 with a failed effort to blow up the statue of Thiers. Lyons was the next target, and in 1883 restaurants, cafés, churches, and parochial schools were hit in a series of bombings similar to attacks in Paris in 1986. In 1886, a bottle of acid was thrown into the Paris stock exchange, and by the early 1890s terrorists had begun to leave bombs that would detonate during the socialist and communist celebration of May Day (May 1) in Paris and other large cities. (Many anarchists opposed the Marxist strategy of taking control of the state through elections.) The bombings discouraged large May Day parades and crowds, but when anarchists were arrested in connection with the 1891 May Day bombings in Paris, fellow anarchists bombed the judge and attorney general who tried to prosecute the terrorists. Anarchists hit their peak activity in France between 1892 and 1894, terrorizing the state and the public with bombings of cafés, police stations, and ultimately, the Chamber of Deputies. President Carnot was murdered in 1893, after which France began a major crackdown on anarchist groups. By the end of the 1890s, police action had put an end to anarchist terror. The anarchists had failed to spark a revolution that would end capitalism and "coercive government" in western Europe. Inside Russia, however, the story was quite different.

Following the assassination of Tsar Alexander II in 1881 by Narodnaya Volia (the People's Will), the police cracked down on the populists and their ideological cousins, the anarchists. Anarchist propaganda circles and secret organizations reappeared in the 1890s (the Anarchist Library, the Geneva Group of Anarchists), smuggling anarchist literature into Russia and agitating among students, workers, and peasants despite attempts by the police to repress their efforts. In 1902, Kropotkin's book *The Conquest of Bread* (*Khleb i Volia*) was published in Russian by an English firm, and an anarchist journal of the same name, *Khleb i Volia*, began circulating the following year (1903). In 1904, before Russia entered a highly unpopular war with Japan, popular discontent was intense and ripe, anarchists reasoned, for "propaganda by the deed." Terrorist bombings began and an editorial in *Khleb i Volia* declared "Only the enemies of the people can be enemies of terror."[31] Government officials, businessmen, and the police were favorite targets, and soon the newspapers were filled with stories of anarchist robberies ("expropriations"), industrial sabotage, and assassinations. The number of anarchist groups increased, especially in the west and south, and their activities ranged from propaganda by the word to leading strikes and robberies to assassination.

Two leading anarchist groups, *Chernoe Znamia* (The Black Banner) and *Beznachalie* (Without Authority), advocated total and ruthless terrorism against capitalists or anyone who worked for the government. Individual acts of terror, mass terror (riots), and economic terror (strikes, robberies, factory bombings) made up their repertoire, and by 1905 instruction manuals for making fire bombs were circulating, too. The terrorism hit its peak toward the end of 1905 when uprisings in several cities threatened to become a full-blown revolution. Tsar Nicholas II was intimidated by a nation convulsed in violence, and he signed the October Manifesto, but the tsar's recognition of popular government and civil rights did not stop the anarchists in their campaign of terror. Nearly five thousand victims[32] died as the terrorism continued for two more years, with an emphasis on bombings (government offices, factories, restaurants, theaters). The move toward a constitutional form of government did not satisfy the anarchists, and the government began to track them down as France had done a decade earlier.

The tsar's prime minister, Stolypin, directed the campaign against the anarchists (who had blown up his home, nearly killing Stolypin's son and daughter). Declaring a state of emergency, the police began hunting down the anarchists. Tried and convicted at the place of their arrest, unless they had committed suicide, the anarchists were quickly suppressed. Their numbers had never been large, but their impact had been great because the anarchists had tapped Russian peasants' and workers' deep animosity toward the government. The surviving anarchists went underground or fled to the West. In hiding or exile, they awaited the next state crisis, World War I.

By 1917, the Russian economy was in shambles and the war against Germany was very unpopular. Anarchists and other revolutionary groups were agitating and organizing resistance, and in February the tsar was forced to hand the state over to a constitutional government. This, of course, did not satisfy the anarchist vision of a revolution, and propaganda by the word and deed continued. Lenin returned to Russia and in his April Theses declared his goals of revolution, ending the war, and abolishing the army and the police. Naturally, this brought many anarchists into a loose alliance with the Bolshevik effort to topple the new government. By November 1917, Russia had a new revolutionary government and within a few months had made a separate peace with the Germans.

The anarchists' mobilization of revolutionary feelings among workers and peasants was important in both revolutions of 1917. The polarization between ruler and ruled had begun in 1905, and the terrorism that marked the struggle twelve years earlier continued past 1917 when anarchists realized that the Bolsheviks had no intention of abolishing the state. Anarchists used violence and terror to resist the Bolsheviks' consolidation of power and were so successful among the peasants that Leon Trotsky was dispatched to lead an army against anarchist leader Nestor Makhno in the south. In time, the anarchists were arrested, exiled, or executed but not before they had succeeded (again) in polarizing popular attitudes toward the government. The anarchists had failed to make the revolutions of 1917 conform to their vision. Because of their hatred of coercion and bureaucracy, they lacked the organization and discipline necessary to take control of the state. They were at a great disadvantage vis-à-vis the Bolsheviks, who eliminated the anarchists as the tsar had done before them. The anarchists had, however, helped alienate the people from their government; the anarchists had further refined the use of terrorism in the course of making a revolution. These two developments were essential features in the revolutions of 1917.

Anarchism and terrorism in Russia perfected two institutions that are central to modern terrorism: (1) the small-group, secret organizational structure that makes terrorism difficult to prevent and (2) "propaganda by the deed." The anarchists' terror had only newspapers and word of mouth to publicize their actions, but word spread quickly. They had meager resources and few members, but the impact of terrorism helped unseat two governments. Elsewhere, the anarchists' terrorism was less successful. In the United States, the Haymarket Riot (1886) and assassination of President McKinley (1901) were as unsuccessful as other anarchist efforts to trigger revolutions in western Europe. Anarchism and terrorism never took root there, never tapped the deep hatred for government felt by Russian peasants and workers. The Russian anarchists and their use of violence to weaken a government represent an important turning point in the evolution of terrorism. By the twentieth century, terrorism had become an ideological weapon that relied on publicity to magnify its impact. The successful use of terrorism to unseat an unpopular and embattled state had been established, and the political philosophy of terror and its tactics had been outlined in the *Revolutionary Catechism*. The impact of groups using terrorism seemed out of proportion to their size and resources. Modern terrorism had emerged and awaited only international travel and communication to become a transnational problem of the twentieth century.

Summary

Terrorism is a very old phenomenon in international politics. Examining its historical record reveals that terrorism also has been a flexible device, useful in governance as well as revolutions and confined to no particular geographic area. One of the oldest accounts of a terrorist campaign is found in Flavius Josephus's history of the Jewish Zealots' efforts to drive the Romans out of Palestine. The Zealots' struggle, which coincided with the birth of Christ, combined nationalism and fanatic religious beliefs to combat (unsuccessfully) the Roman Empire.

Terrorism first entered our political vocabulary when Edmund Burke criticized the "reign of terror" in the French Revolution. Between 1792 and 1794, the French government systematically used terror to intimidate or eliminate the "enemies of the revolution." Fear of the guillotine became the principle instrument of state terror, enabling the government to suppress a civil war and a counterrevolution. The French government justified its use of terrorism as necessary if the state were to survive. This raison d'état will appear again in the examination of twentieth-century terrorism.

Terrorism's historical flexibility has a third dimension. In addition to its usefulness in struggles for national liberation and its role in state self-defense, terrorism has old ties to radical ideologies that exalt violence as a means to promote revolutionary change in the state. Russian anarchists in nineteenth-century Europe, for example, combined a belief in revolutionary violence with secret terrorist cells and "propaganda of the deed" to magnify the impact of violence through secret organizations and publicity. That legacy is visible in most terrorist operations today.

Terrorism is a flexible device: it can be used by or against groups or governments and for any number of political objectives. Terrorism's history is long and reveals a phenomenon that has become increasingly common and flexible over time.

3
Terrorism and Nationalism

Terrorism is an old and flexible instrument for accomplishing political goals. Zealots used terrorism nineteen hundred years ago trying to drive the Romans out of Palestine. The French Revolution passed through a phase in which the ruling clique used terrorism to eliminate or intimidate opponents of the Revolution. Anarchists in nineteenth-century Europe further refined the philosophy of terrorism, which they called Propaganda by the Deed, as they tried to instigate radical political change through sensational acts of violence. One of the most enduring sources of terrorism has been nationalism, which often produces the desire for national liberation or national self-determination, along with a willingness to use violence to accomplish such a goal. Nationalism grows out of a group's special sense of shared identity, which may be based on race, religion, language, territory, culture, or ethnicity. That shared identity often distinguishes the group from its neighbors, creating differences that may lead to political conflict. Such conflict often convinces the group that to survive and preserve its identity, the group must be autonomous and operate as an independent nation-state. The desire for autonomy or national liberation has been and remains today one of the most potent and lethal sources of terrorism.

In this chapter five cases of terrorism that are rooted in struggles for national liberation are reviewed. The oldest ongoing source of terrorism, the clash of Irish and British nationalisms, is discussed first, followed by the cases of Armenian, Palestinian, Sikh, and Basque uses of terrorism to promote the cause of national liberation. All five cases involve the clash of cultures, religions, and the politics of state building versus group autonomy. These five cases hold the promise of ongoing conflict and resort to terrorism. All five cases have spilled over national boundaries to qualify as international terrorism, and each case continues to tap the emotions and energy of nationalism.

Terrorism in Northern Ireland

> The IRA fought the guerrilla war of 1919–21 and was the midwife of the nation-state. By destroying British administration in nationalist Ireland the IRA in 30 months accomplished what the Parliamentary Party had failed to do in 50 years: it forced a settlement of the Irish question.[1]

Terrorism in Northern Ireland today is the direct descendant of the clash between Irish and British nationalisms dating back over eight hundred years. Since that time, terrorism, sabotage, pogroms, guerrilla warfare, civil war, and interstate war have marked Anglo-Irish relations. Violence, especially terrorism, continues to afflict the people of Northern Ireland today. The conflict that generates terrorism in Northern Ireland is the result of a struggle over who will control Ireland: the British or the Irish? Anglo-Normans arrived in Ireland in A.D. 1169, and two years later English King Henry II himself came to Ireland to conquer the Normans and the Gaelic peoples. (Pope Adrian V had awarded Henry II a much-debated papal grant to rule Ireland.) Ireland absorbed most of the cronies that Henry II established on confiscated Irish lands and the plague of 1348 decimated the rest. In 1500, King Henry VII set out to reestablish English control of Ireland, and in 1534 Henry VIII added a new dimension to the Anglo-Irish conflict when he broke with Rome. Ireland remained Roman Catholic, but by the end of the century Protestant Scots and English settlers began arriving in increasing numbers in Ireland to colonize the early "plantations." Ulster's settlements on confiscated land coincided with the founding of Jamestown in the New World, and the descendants of the Protestant colonists in Ulster today feel they have the right to be in Ireland and to remain under British rule. The seeds planted centuries ago continue to bear fruit today.

English rule in Ireland in the sixteenth and seventeenth centuries was harsh, particularly under Cromwell, but Irish Catholics were set against and apart from Protestants most clearly by the Penal Laws beginning in 1709. Catholics could not vote, belong to corporations, serve as lawyers or judges or police, own guns, receive an education, or buy or inherit land. A series of revolts began and secret societies were set up to preserve Irish culture as well as promote revolution and republican philosophy. When they received suffrage, Irish Catholics also elected members to Parliament and demanded Home Rule (1870).

The Easter Rising of 1916 set into motion five years of terrorism and guerrilla warfare, part of the revolutionary struggle led by the Irish Republican Army (IRA). The culmination of the struggle came in 1921 with the Anglo-Irish Treaty: twenty-six counties in the south became the Irish Free State, while six counties in the northeast, part of Ulster province, were partitioned to become Northern Ireland. Northern Ireland was two-thirds Protestant, and the six counties (Antrim, Armagh, Derry, Down, Fermanaugh, and Tyrone) became a Protestant state for Protestants. Catholics there would face employment, housing, and other forms of discrimination in the years to follow.

The IRA rejected partition when terms of the 1921 treaty were announced and has fought for reunification of Ireland since that time. The IRA led a civil war for two years following the treaty, unsuccessfully demanding complete British withdrawal from the island. The IRA efforts were defeated by the Free State Army led by Michael Collins. Since that time, the IRA has directed its efforts to reunify Ireland toward Great Britain. To that end, the IRA conducted its "bombs for Britain" campaign in 1938 and 1939, hoping to force the British government to negotiate an end to partition. Bombs went off in the London Underground (train system), at Victoria Station and at Piccadilly Circus. Liverpool, Manchester, Coventry, and Birmingham were also targets of bombings, which always were preceded by a warning. When investigators found a copy of the bombing plans, word leaked to the press and public alarm reached even greater heights. The tear gas and gelignite bomb squads all were caught or fled England, and the onset of World War II distracted the public and the government from the IRA's demands and the tensions in Northern Ireland.

From 1956 to 1962 the IRA conducted another terror campaign but shifted its focus from England to the border between the Free State and Northern Ireland. The IRA still believed that only violence would lead to British withdrawal and Irish reunification, and border police and customs officers were targeted for ambushes and bombings. British military barracks were raided for weapons, and "Operation Harvest" began, embodying IRA hopes to challenge Great Britain directly on the site of their dispute. Like the earlier campaign of 1938–1939, the operation failed and most of the IRA personnel involved found themselves in jail. The IRA and a new "provisional" wing would not participate actively again in Northern Ireland politics until the fledgling civil rights movement and the Catholic community came under attack by Protestant paramilitary terrorist groups in 1969.

Influenced by the civil rights movement in the United States, which publicized and peacefully protested against racial discrimination, the Northern Ireland Civil Rights Association (NICRA) was established in 1967. NICRA shared some of its membership with the Wolfe Tone Society (established in 1963), which consisted of Protestants and Catholics, communists, socialists, and republicans who were concerned about rights issues, especially laws against republicanism and the Special Powers Act and Offenses against the State Act. (Those acts allowed the government, among other things, to detain suspected political offenders without charge or trial.) NICRA focused on economic and religious discrimination against Catholics in Northern Ireland, particularly unemployment, housing discrimination, and gerrymandered underrepresentation of Catholics in Stormont, the northern Irish government. Opponents of the NICRA accused it of being a front for the IRA, others believed that the IRA supported the civil rights movement because the IRA itself had accepted the failure of armed resistance. After declaring itself a socialist organization in 1968 and calling for economic and political struggle to enhance the likelihood of armed success, the IRA fully supported the NICRA.

In August 1968, the first of many peace marches by the NICRA took place. Over three thousand people assembled in Belfast to demand economic and religious equality, singing "We Shall Overcome." The following year, a march from Belfast to Derry (Londonderry) was planned, modeled after Dr. Martin Luther King's march from Selma to Montgomery, Alabama. The marchers were ambushed near Derry by a Protestant vigilante group that followed the violent, sectarian teachings of Reverend Ian Paisley; police joined the vigilantes in assaulting the marchers. The United Kingdom sent more troops to Northern Ireland, and the socialist IRA suffered a split as the Provisional-IRA separated to pursue the traditional, republican demands:

1. U.K. withdrawal from Ireland,

2. Amnesty for political prisoners, and

3. Reunification of Ireland.

As the community became more polarized, the number of Protestant paramilitary vigilante groups increased (Ulster Volunteer Force, Ulster Defense Association, Ulster Freedom Fighters, Red Hand Commandos). The "Provos" undertook to protect Catholic areas where the police (Royal Ulster Constabulary) were not trusted. Car bombings, snipers, arson, and assassinations had Belfast in chaos, with armed groups attacking each other and the citizenry. London finally decided in March 1972 to abolish local rule (Stormont) and govern Northern Ireland directly.

Since the mid-1970s, the traditional terrorist struggle has continued, comprised now of Protestant vigilante groups, the traditional (non-Marxist) Provisional IRA, and the socialist Irish National Liberation Army (INLA). Terrorism is employed in Northern Ireland, Great Britain, and abroad. The vigilante Protestant groups have used terrorism to intimidate Ulster Catholics and threats of civil war to paralyze two Anglo-Irish efforts (Sunningdale Conference on Power Sharing, 1973, and the Hillsborough Agreement, 1985) devoted to the reunification and economic rehabilitation of the island. The Provisional IRA and INLA continue to use terrorism to pressure Britain into withdrawal from Ireland.

The INLA assassinated the leading Conservative spokesman for Northern Ireland, Airey Neave, in London in 1979 and also killed Protestant, leader John McDeague in Belfast in 1981. The Provos have conducted a series of bombings and assassinations since the official IRA declared a cease-fire with the British in 1972. The Provisional IRA placed bombs in Westminster Hall in 1974 and Hyde Park in 1982, killing royal mounted guardsmen; Lord Mountbatten and the British ambassador to Holland were assassinated in 1979, and an attempt was made on the life of Prime Minister Margaret Thatcher in 1984 during a Conservative Party Conference (a bomb was set in the Grand Hotel in Brighton where Thatcher was staying). The Provos have attacked British Army of the Rhine personnel in Germany and also have attacked government representatives to the Common Market in Brussels and private British businesses across Europe. The strategy is consistent with the long-held belief that only force will convince Britain to put an end to its presence in Ireland. Simultaneously, groups have emerged from the Protestant community using terrorism to force the British to stay to keep the peace and prevent civil war.

The Provisional IRA and INLA use terrorism to promote the cause of reunification of the Irish people. Protestant paramilitary groups in Northern Ireland use terrorism to prevent such reunification, insisting on their right to remain British. The clash of national identities in Ulster, British versus Irish, compounded by religious and economic conflicts, seems likely to continue as the most long-standing site of terrorism in international politics.

Terrorism and the Armenians

Who after all speaks today of the annihilation of the Armenians?[2]

In 1973, young Armenian terrorists set out to remind Armenians, Turkey, and the international community of their desire for an independent Armenian state. The Turkish consul general was assassinated in Santa Barbara, California, in 1973 and over the course of the following decade and a half Armenian terrorists would strike targets in twenty-two different countries across the Middle East, Europe, North America, and Australia. By 1975, two organizations had emerged to lead the struggle for an Armenian homeland: the Armenian Secret Army for the Liberation of Armenia (ASALA) and the Justice Commandos of the Armenian Genocide (JCAG). Both organizations operated out of the Armenian community in Beirut where violence had become the last remaining means of getting attention. They were inspired by radical Palestinian groups that had turned to terrorism to draw attention to their grievances and demands. ASALA, representing left-wing Armenian youth and JCAG, representing the right-wing of the movement, targeted Turkish diplomats, embassies, and airlines in order to publicize Turkish atrocities in 1915–1916 against Armenians and their demand for an autonomous homeland. (There is an Armenian republic in the Soviet Union, but the bulk of the Armenian people are expatriate and many consider the eastern region of Turkey to be their rightful "homeland.")

Armenian terrorism has claimed Turkish diplomats as victims in Athens, Beirut, Belgrade, Bern, Brussels, Geneva, The Hague, Lisbon, Los Angeles, Madrid, Ottawa, Paris, Rome, Sydney, Vatican City, and Vienna. In 1981, at the height of its activity to date, ASALA claimed responsibility for forty attacks in eleven different countries.[3] The Turkish national airline, THY, has had its offices in Amsterdam, Copenhagen, Frankfurt, Geneva, London, Milan, Paris, and Rome bombed, and the Turkish delegation to the Organization for Economic Cooperation and Development (OECD) and the Turkish Center at the United Nations have also been bombed. This sudden and extreme burst of international activity on behalf of Armenian nationalism can be traced back to events in 1915 and 1916, which are the bases of Armenian demands and their desire for publicity for the "forgotten genocide." The outburst in the 1970s was inspired by the political turmoil in Beirut and the Palestinian example.

During the course of World War I, the Turkish government carried out a policy to relocate and neutralize the threat believed posed by the Armenian community in Turkey. Armenians residing in Russia were fighting with the Russian army against Turkey, and expatriate Armenians were fighting with several other belligerent states. The relocation effort, according to U.S. Ambassador Henry Morgenthau, was not intended to reestablish Armenians outside strategic areas but to exterminate them. Thousands of Armenians had died in government sanctioned massacres in 1894–1896 and 1909, and the 1915–1916 deportations were so well documented that the French coined the phrase "crimes against humanity"[4] to describe Turkish policy at the time. The Turkish government insists that approximately three hundred thousand Armenians died as a result of the war. Armenians claim between 1 and 2 million Armenians died as a result of executions or forced marches into the Syrian desert (without water, food, or shelter). The Turkish government has published a large body of literature disproving or denying the "genocide," and a central feature of Armenian terrorism is to reestablish the memory of the Armenians' holocaust. Second, the Armenian groups also claim the right to exact revenge on Turkey, which committed atrocities and then alledgedly tried to cover them up.

The special identity of Armenians as a people and a nation, separate from Turkey by virtue of Armenian culture and their Christian faith is a key element in Armenian nationalism. The vulnerability of Armenians who could not rely on the protection of a national government became obvious after World War I. In the Treaty of Sevres (1920), the victorious Europeans provided for the creation of an independent Armenia, but failed to follow through on that commitment. The Armenians who survived World War I (250,000 in the United States; 32,000 in Turkey; 4 million in various other states[5]) now have organizations, particularly ASALA, that demand an Armenian nation-state to protect and preserve the Armenian people and culture. Terrorism has proven useful in (1) publicizing the 1915–1916 genocide, (2) counteracting Turkish denials, (3) obtaining revenge, and (4) establishing for the international record the desire for an Armenian homeland. The young Armenian population in Beirut, who observed for themselves the Palestinian diaspora and resort to terrorism in the 1960s and 1970s, chose terrorism as the only available means to publicize and press Armenian demands. The immediate prospects, however, of Turkey acceding to Armenian demands for reparations and a homeland are poor. Turkey continues to publish literature discounting the alleged genocide and portrays Armenian demands as part of a Soviet-backed effort to weaken the NATO alliance. Meanwhile, ASALA continues to conduct "propaganda by the deed," drawing attention to the Armenian cause through acts of terrorism. Prospects remain poor for reconciliation of this conflict between the aspirations of Armenian nationalism and a Turkish state that must govern a multiethnic society. The acts of international terrorism, most of which occur outside Turkey, are the result of a frustrated nationalism and a desire for revenge; the terrorism will probably continue into the foreseeable future.

Palestinian Nationalism and Terrorism

> When we looked around us we could see either the desert to shed our tears in or the whole world to hit back at. Having nothing and with nothing to lose, we proceeded to do the latter.[6]

The clash between Palestinians and Israelis over the land they know, respectively, as Palestine and Eretz Israel dates back fourteen hundred years before the birth of Christ. Hebrews and Philistines struggled for control of Canaan, as it was known then; their struggle continues today, in and outside Israel. U.S. Secretary of State Henry Kissinger, reflecting on the 1973 Arab-Israeli war, described the Israeli-Palestinian struggle as the clash of two rights, the rights of both peoples to self-determination and their own nation-state. Terrorism has played an ongoing role in their struggle, especially since World War II and the formation of the Jewish state of Israel in 1948. Like the case of terrorism in Northern Ireland and Armenians use of terrorism, the Palestinians' resort to terrorism is intricately linked with historical developments in Palestine/Israel.

In A.D. 70 the Romans destroyed the Jewish temple in Jerusalem and in A.D. 135 most Jews were dispersed from Palestine, beginning the Jewish diaspora, the wanderings of a stateless people. The Palestinian people remained in Palestine, where their country was conquered or ruled by successive empires (Arabic, Christian crusaders, Ottoman Turkish, and British). Without a country of their own and scattered across the Middle East, Northern Africa, and Europe, Jews suffered discrimination and persecution. Despite those hardships, Jews retained their special identity, preserving their religion and reviving their spoken language, Hebrew. In 1896, Theodore Herzl wrote *The Jewish State*, and the Zionist movement to reestablish a Jewish state in Palestine began in earnest. Jews began emigrating to Palestine, and in 1917 the Balfour Declaration publicly announced Britain's support for a Jewish national homeland in Palestine. Arabs, including Palestinians, protested the concept and the continuing Jewish immigration; terrorism between Arabs and Jews began to occur in this early phase of Jewish return to Palestine.

In 1920, after promising Arabs independence in exchange for their help in the war against the Ottoman Empire, Britain accepted a League of Nations mandate over Palestine, Jordan, and Iraq. Arabs did not receive independence, Jewish immigration continued (three hundred thousand from 1920 to 1939), and violence escalated between Arabs and Jews in Palestine. Hitler's rise to power (1933) intensified the persecution of Jews in Europe and the pressure to emigrate. Palestinians staged a national strike in 1936 to protest British policy permitting Jewish immigration, and the strike became an armed rebellion, which British troops quelled in 1939. To prevent further unrest, and to encourage Arab support in the war against Germany, Britain limited further Jewish immigration to Palestine. During World War II Zionist groups organized illegal immigration to Palestine for over two hundred thousand European Jews. When the war ended in 1945, violent clashes broke out between immigrant Jews and Palestinian Arabs. Britain, prostrate after its exertions in World War II, informed the new United Nations that it would terminate British control of the Mandate areas. While the United Nations prepared a plan to establish independent Palestinian and Jewish states, terrorism increased. Jewish immigrants had organized *Haganah* (defense) in the 1920s in response to terrorist attacks on settlers, and *Irgun Zvai Leumi* was formed in the 1930s (headed by Menahem Begin) for similar reasons. Irgun and the Stern Gang led terrorist attacks on British forces and Palestinians as the situation deteriorated. When the British departed Israel in 1948, Jews declared the establishment of a Jewish state and immediately were attacked by Egypt, Jordan, Syria, Iraq, and Lebanon. The new state of Israel was successfully defended, its territory expanded beyond the borders the United Nations had planned, and nearly a million Palestinians became refugees. In 1956, *FATAH* (*Harakat al-Tahir al-Filastiniya* or Palestinian Liberation Movement) was established by expatriate Palestinians to promote "the expression of the Palestinian people and of its will to free its land from Zionist colonization in order to recover its national identity."[7] Until the Six-Day War of 1967 when Israel further enlarged the territory under its control (adding the West Bank, East Jerusalem, Gaza Strip, Sinai Desert, and Golan Heights), the Palestinians' aspirations for an independent Palestinian state had been supervised by their Arab hosts. Hope for a return to Palestine lay with Arab leaders like Gamal Nasser of Egypt, where the creation of the Palestine Liberation Organization (PLO) had been arranged. After the stunning victory of Israel in 1967 and the humiliation of their Arab sponsors, Palestinians took their fate into their own hands. *FATAH*, which had staged its first terrorist operation inside Israel in 1965, filled the void left by the defeat of the Arab armies. *FATAH*, led by Yasir Arafat, organized a movement by guerrilla groups and seized control of the PLO.

The decade that followed was marked by attacks in and outside Israel and by sensational acts of international terrorism (e.g., hijackings and the 1972 Munich Olympics attack) to publicize Palestinians' grievances and demands. The Palestinians use of international terrorism derived from three factors. First, traditional military encounters and guerrilla attacks in Israel (or the Occupied Territories) have nearly always been crushed by the superbly trained Israeli Defense Forces (IDF) and Israeli intelligence forces. Second, since the 1973 Yom Kippur War and the 1982 invasion of Lebanon, Israel has secured its borders, and access to Israel proper has been curtailed dramatically. (In 1979, Israel signed a peace treaty with Egypt and returned control of the Sinai desert. In 1981, Israel annexed the Golan Heights where the Israeli and Syrian borders meet. In 1983 Israel set up a 20 kilometer demilitarized zone on its border with Lebanon. Israel continues to occupy and settle the West Bank, bordering Jordan.) Palestinians find it easier to strike at Israelis outside Israel, or at friends of Israel, especially the United States.

Third, Palestinians are deeply divided over the appropriate strategy for defeating Israel and establishing a Palestinian state. The number of Palestinian liberation groups has multiplied, and many have resorted to terrorism to publicize their organization and attract members from the numerous Palestinian refugee camps in Lebanon, Syria, and Jordan. Terrorism is sometimes used against rival groups. Abu Nidal (who led the 1985 bombings of the Rome and Vienna airports, and the assassination attempt on the life of the Israeli ambassador to Britain in 1982) broke with Arafat and *FATAH* in 1973 and tried to have Arafat assassinated. Many groups are sponsored by rival Arab states (Syria, Iraq, Iran, and Libya) that have their own reasons for sponsoring Palestinian terrorism.

Although Palestinian terrorism has not destroyed Israel or forced the

Israelis to trade "land for peace," terrorist violence has attracted international attention and some support. In 1974 the PLO was recognized as the "sole, legitimate representative of the Palestinian people" and was granted permanent observer status at the United Nations. The United Nations condemned Zionism as a form of racism, and the Arab oil embargo of 1973–1974 brought even more supporters to the Palestinian movement.

Palestinian terrorism is rooted in a desire to provide a national homeland for the stateless Palestinian people and also in the frustation of forty years of unsuccessful struggle against Israel. The number of Palestinian groups that resort to terrorism continues to grow. Among the primary groups struggling for dominance of the movement are

1. *FATAH*: Arafat's base organization, which hopes to liberate Palestine through low-intensity warfare. *FATAH* has a nationalist ideology.
2. PFLP (Popular Front for the Liberation of Palestine): Led by Dr. George Habash, the PFLP adheres to a Marxist-Leninist ideology and is the major rival of *FATAH*. The PFLP rejects any form of negotiation or compromise with Israel. Splinter groups include DPFLP (Democratic Popular Front for the Liberation of Palestine), the PFLP-General Command and the OAP (Organization of Arab Palestine).
3. *Saiqa* (Thunderbolt): A Syrian based and sponsored group that is militaristic and nationalistic and specializes in attacks in the Golan Heights and the West Bank.

Despite the proliferation of groups and their rivalry (which often leads to violence), nearly all the Palestinian organizations subscribe to the PLO Charter of 1968, which expresses a commitment to armed struggle and national action. The failure of the orthodox military struggle and the resort to terrorism have been key developments in the Israeli-Palestinian struggle. At the center of the conflict, however, is the issue of which nationality will control the very small parcel of real estate once known as Palestine and now called Israel. As in the case of Northern Ireland, numerous efforts to negotiate a peaceful settlement of the conflict have failed. The struggle and the terrorism are likely to continue indefinitely.

Terrorism and Sikh Nationalism

The Sikh community's struggle for autonomy attracted world attention in October 1984 when Indian Prime Minister Indira Gandhi was assassinated by two Sikh bodyguards. Gandhi was murdered for ordering the Indian army to attack the Sikhs' Golden Temple, their holiest shrine, which had been turned into an armory for radical Sikh nationalists. Before the Indian army beseiged the Golden Temple, Sikh terrorists had killed over a hundred people in 1983 and nearly three hundred people in 1984. The attack on the Golden Temple (code name: Operation Blue Star) lasted three days. When it ended, over five hundred people were dead, including Sant Jarnail Singh Bhindranwale, the leader of the terrorist movement for an independent Sikh homeland. The violence, however, would continue inside India and abroad.

India, like other states facing nationalist terrorism from minority groups, has citizens of many languages, cultures, and religions. The Sikh people (15 million of India's 800 million) practice a religion founded in the fifteenth century, a faith that weaves together elements from Islam and Hinduism. Sikhs also reject the Indian caste system. The Sikhs live in the Punjab region of India (when it was partitioned in 1947 between India and Pakistan, most Sikhs chose to live in India). The Sikhs have the cultural traditions of a "warrior race" stemming from repeated invasions of the Punjab, which came to be called the shield, spear, and sword hand of India. Today, the special identity of Sikhs is manifested in the continuing struggle for an autonomous Sikh homeland called Khalistan, the Land of the Pure. Sikh nationalists in the Dal Khalsa movement, which promotes the idea of an independent Khalistan, believe that their regional, cultural, and economic interests cannot be maximized in an Indian state dominated by Hindu and upper-caste political interests. Under the British Raj, the Sikhs had attained the right to supervise their religious shrines, a Sikh university was established, and Sikhs had a powerful voice in the Punjab legislature. The seeds of autonomy were planted and nourished by the British who were trying to prevent Mohandas Gandhi from unifying the people of the subcontinent in a revolutionary movement to end British rule. When India and Pakistan became sovereign, independent states in 1947, India inherited a Sikh community with grievances, the sense of being a threatened minority, and aspirations for autonomy.

The Akali Dal party agitated for a Sikh province to shelter and promote Sikh religion and culture. In 1966, the Indian state acquiesced and a separate state with a Sikh majority was created. In 1973, the Sikh community demanded even greater control of regional affairs; under the Anandpur Sahib Resolution, New Delhi would control only defense, foreign affairs, currency, communications, and transportation issues. While the central government stalled, a powerful, charismatic figure began arguing that only an independent Khalistan could preserve and purify the Sikh community. Sant (saint) Bhindranwale, born the same year India became independent, was considered a fundamentalist by his co-religionists and a fanatic extremist by the Indian government. Increasingly an advocate of violence, Bhindranwale became more militant, and his followers carried out a series of assassinations that included the Indian deputy police inspector general.

Prime Minister Gandhi, like the British in Northern Ireland, was forced to govern the Punjab directly.

Bhindranwale's influence and the violence that accompanied it did not diminish, and the repressive measures Gandhi imposed only drove moderate Sikhs into the extremist camp. When she learned that Shahbeg Singh (a retired major-general of India's army) was training Sikh terrorists and fortifying the Golden Temple at Amritsar, Gandhi ordered the army to assault the shrine in June 1984. Shahbeg Singh had done his work well; the Indian army needed three days, tanks, and artillery to rout the Sikh nationalists from the Golden Temple. Shahbeg Singh and Sant Bhindranwale both died in the seige, martyrs for the cause of Khalistan. The Sikh community was horrified at the violation of their holiest shrine, which destroyed a major arsenal but did not destroy Sikh terrorism. Plans to avenge the insult took shape quickly, and Indira Gandhi lay dead four months later, machine-gunned by two Sikh bodyguards.

Since the assassination and the anti-Sikh riots that followed it, the Sikh community has grown more alienated from the Indian government. Sikh terrorists continue to train and operate in both the Punjab and abroad (Britain has a large Sikh community); the most lethal attack has been the bombing of an Air India flight from Canada, which crashed off the coast of Ireland in June 1985, killing all 329 people aboard. The Indian government has resumed discussions of Sikh autonomy but is reluctant to reduce central government control of a state located on the border with both the People's Republic of China and Pakistan.

Meanwhile, India confronts the problem of a violent separatist Tamil minority in neighboring Sri Lanka. The Tamils have many relatives and Hindu co-religionists in India, and the Indian government does not want to offend 50 million Tamils in India by ignoring the separatist/nationalist movement in Sri Lanka. The Indian government wrestles with Sikh demands in the light of Punjab's strategic location and with a concern to balance Sikh and Tamil demands. The capacity for violence in these separatist causes will continue to challenge the authority of the multi-ethnic Indian state, making resolution of the conflicts difficult and a quick end to the terrorism unlikely.

Basque Nationals and Terrorism

Actions Unite. Words Divide.
— ETA slogan (1968)

The Basques are one of Europe's oldest peoples, and their history of invasion by outsiders has produced a tradition of resisting any power that tries to limit Basque autonomy. Today, their struggle lies with the Spanish government, which used terror and torture during the Franco regime in an attempt to crush Basque nationalism. The Basques responded by creating *Euzkadi Ta Askatasuna* (Basque Homeland and Freedom) or ETA, which has focused a campaign of terror against the Spanish government, especially the police and armed forces. Having set out to liberate the Basque homeland by force, the militant wing of ETA now rejects overtures from Franco's successors, overtures that offer a large measure of autonomy for the Basque people. The desire for independence is too old and entrenched in Basque culture to trust the offers of the fledgling democratic government in Madrid. The terror machine, although small, appears to be too well organized and too popular to disappear easily.

No one knows how old the Basques are, or how they came to Europe. The Basque language—Euzkera—is also a mystery, and it is one of the most distinctive features of their culture. (Franco tried to eliminate the teaching of the language.) The Basques are of pre-Celtic origins and settled in what are now four Spanish and three French provinces along the Pyrennees mountains. The Basques may have been in Europe for over twenty thousand years, and during that time they have endured conquests by the Romans, Visigoths, and Islamic warriors. From the Visigoths the Basques took the traditions of feudal laws and regionalism—for a king to gain homage from the Basques he had to recognize and respect their feudal laws. In other words, an outsider conquering the Basques had to accept their laws and customs, the essence of self-determination. This tradition helped the Basques maintain their separate identity as a people with territorial autonomy and a special culture all their own.

In 1895, the Basque Nationalist Party (PNV) was established to promote the Basque language and nationalism, but the PNV was ineffective in resisting the persecution of Basques under the Franco regime after the Spanish Civil War (1936–1939). Franco's assault on Basque traditions included policies to repress the speaking and teaching of Euzkera and the imprisonment and torture of Basque nationalists. In 1950, a study group of Basque university students began discussing the repression and the PNV's failure to resist the government's policies. ETA was the child of the study group, organized officially in 1959 as a political party committed to establishing an independent Basque homeland. ETA split into several factions, including a political wing and a secret, armed organization to punish and terrorize the police and security forces that had brutalized Basques on Franco's orders. The impotence of the PNV would soon be forgotten.

ETA began a campaign of terror in 1968 with attacks on the Spanish police. The strategy was simple: to exploit the deep resentment Basques felt toward the Spanish government by attacking the agents of the state, forcing the government to respond with even more repressive policies. ETA hoped Basques would see that the police were vulnerable and that the government would always be repressive. This would then trigger greater popular resistance, the theory contended, and lead to Basque independence. In December 1973, ETA added government officials to its list of targets by assassinating Prime Minister Admiral Luis Carrero Blanco. (Since that time over fifty senior officers in the Spanish military have died in ETA attacks.) In 1978, ETA repeated its claim that peaceful change was impossible, and thirty-nine Spanish police and military officers died in attacks the following year in Basque areas and in Madrid. In the 1980s, ETA has continued to focus on the rank and file police force as its preferred target, but the target list has been diversified. The commander of the provincial police in Alava (a Basque area) and his deputy were assassinated in 1980. In 1982, the Madrid telephone exchange was bombed, causing $20 million in damage and great social disruption. In 1985 and 1986, ETA expanded the scope of its attacks by bombing numerous tourist resorts in Spain, putting new pressures on the government. General Miguel Quintana (1984), General Juan Atares (1985), and Vice Admiral Cristobal Colon (1986) were assassinated, as well, keeping ETA in the Spanish headlines.

Many parallels have been drawn between ETA and the Provisional IRA. Both organizations oppose compromise partial settlement of their demands for national independence. Both movements have benefited from a long, open border with a friendly neighbor. ETA terrorists have long enjoyed a political refuge in France, with its tradition of providing safe haven to revolutionaries. France and the Provo-IRA have also been a source of arms, explosives, and funding for ETA, and Basques reportedly have trained with their Northern Irish colleagues in Algeria, Lebanon, and South Yemen. Like the Provisional IRA, ETA has recently begun to attack commercial as well as political targets. In June 1987, a car bomb exploded in the underground parking garage of a Barcelona department store, killing fifteen and injuring forty people.

ETA's threat is present throughout Spain, hitting security forces, government officials, businesses, and tourist spots. The independence movement, radicalized by Franco's brutal repression, is unable or unwilling to engage the new, democratic government in a dialogue on autonomy. In 1978, the PNV accepted the new regime's constitution, which granted greater autonomy to Basque regions; ETA, however, rejected the Constitution and adopted more radical and violent methods to obtain complete independence. The continuing terrorism creates a serious dilemma for the Spanish state. The government wants peace and democracy, but it also wants to preserve the unity of Spain as a whole. ETA terrorism may force the government to choose between peace and unity. The radical, militant wing of ETA seems convinced that there can be no peaceful resolution of the clash between Basque and Spanish nationalisms.

Summary

Frustrated ambitions for national autonomy are among the most potent dynamics that produce terrorism today. Nationalism, when it occurs in a religious or ethnic community, often threatens the legitimacy and security of multi-ethnic states. Those states, like the United Kingdom, Turkey, Israel, India, and Spain, confront serious political problems if they ignore *or* if they negotiate demands for autonomy. This is one reason why the five cases examined here have been prolonged for generations. Terrorism has persisted and national liberation groups have proliferated, while governments pursue counterterrorism strategies that rarely address underlying, nationalistic motivations. Groups that resort to terrorism have little trouble finding sponsors, and violence seems to acquire the capacity to perpetuate itself in a cycle of grievances and revenge. All contribute to the enduring and ubiquitous problem of international terrorism, driven by the engine of nationalism.

4
State Terrorism

Terrorism is a flexible and ubiquitous method used since ancient times in struggles for national liberation. Terrorism also has been used by governments to repress and intimidate groups or movements that challenge the state's security. State terrorism further reveals how readily adaptable terrorism is, regardless of the time, place, or purpose for which it is used. Terrorism may be used by groups to topple states, and it may also be used by governments against individuals or groups. In this chapter what may be the most frightening form of terrorism, governance by terror, will be discussed.

The twentieth century has witnessed many examples of state terrorism. These cases have seen governments use violence against symbolic targets for political reasons, with two additional features that only governments can bring to terrorism: bureaucratic calculation and the use of the police and the armed forces. State terrorism has a particularly bureaucratic flavor in its systematic execution, and it is made even more horrifying by the participation of the police, or security forces. No one is left to protect the public when the state uses the military or the police as an instrument of terror. This magnifies the fear generated by state terrorism in much the same manner that media coverage brings home the immediate danger of antistate terrorism.

Nazi Germany established the general pattern that modern state terrorism follows. On coming to power in 1933, Adolph Hitler demanded control of the Ministry of the Interior in exchange for his participation in the coalition government. That ministry included the German police, and Hitler also continued to build his own army and security forces to terrorize his political opponents (especially communists) and the Jewish community. Throughout the 1930s, the Nazis used the police and the bureaucracy to harass and attack the state's internal "enemies." After 1941 the state's terrorism became even more systematic and deadly: the "Final Solution" was adopted, and the plan to eradicate permanently the enemies of National Socialism got underway. The twin terrors of Nazism and the Holocaust culminated in the deaths of 6 million Jews, the symbolic target of Hitler's philosophy of hatred. Another 16 million[1] Poles, Russians, and Gypsies also died in Nazi captivity, victims of the machinery of state terrorism that combined bureaucratic thoroughness with the instruments of violence and destruction.

The state terrorism of Nazi Germany is the most widely known and documented example of its kind, although its scope may have been matched by Joseph Stalin's atrocities in the Soviet Union. Alexander Solzhenitsyn, the expatriate Soviet writer, has argued that Stalin used the KGB and the bureaucracy (courts, prisons, etc.) to terrorize, purge, and destroy over 15 million peasants, communists, prisoners of war, and ethnic nationals between 1929 and 1946.[2] The terror intimidated the general population, which found no way to resist the unpredictable violence committed by the state. Modern examples of state terrorism have not equaled the magnitude of the Nazi holocaust or Stalin's genocides, but state terrorism also has not abated. After an aborted coup d'état in Indonesia in October 1965, the government conducted massive waves of arrests and executions of communists. Between two hundred thousand and 1 million[3] are estimated to have died, while the general population was terrorized into silence. Idi Amin Dada, Ugandan President for Life, terrorized his people from 1971 to 1979 using the state security forces to abduct, torture, and murder political critics and opponents. Pol Pot and the Khmer Rouge terrorized Cambodia (Kampuchea) from 1975 to 1979 in order to destroy dissent and restructure society into a communist utopia. Idi Amin may have killed one hundred thousand to five hundred thousand in Uganda;[4] 2 million[5] may have died on Cambodia's "killing fields." In both countries, those who did not become victims of the state's terror had to wait for outside forces to halt the violence. Vietnam invaded Kampuchea and halted the killing machine in December 1978; Tanzania invaded Uganda in April 1979 and overthrew Idi Amin with the help of Ugandan guerrillas.

State terrorism continues to become more sophisticated in its use of violence against individuals or groups who threaten the government's sense of security. The next sections will focus on two modern cases of state terrorism, one left-wing and the other right-wing, in which the machinery of internal state violence has reached new levels of efficiency and lethality. The Argentine "dirty war" against "subversive elements" (1976–1983) and the Soviet Union's use of psychiatry to intimidate and terrorize dissidents (especially dissidents among the intelligensia) are considered next.

Argentina's "Dirty War" and "the Disappeared"

First we will kill all the subversives; then we will kill their collaborators; then . . . their sympathizers, then . . . those who remain indifferent; and finally we will kill the timid.[6]

In the autumn of 1984, the Argentine National Commission on Disappeared Persons (CODEP) issued its report on what had happened in Argentina between 1976 and 1983. During the long nightmare, known as the "Process of National Reorganization" under the military junta that ruled Argentina, the government conducted a "dirty war" against terrorists and subversives. CODEP reported that 340 clandestine jails and torture centers operated during the dirty war, and 8,961 prisoners[7] are still unaccounted for and missing. High-ranking military officers have testified that the junta was committed to waging war on terrorists and communists, not only to defeat the subversive elements but to eliminate them, once and for all, from Argentine society. (Five of the original nine military junta leaders have been convicted of ordering the kidnapping, torture, and murder of Argentine citizens. Four heads of state security agencies have also been convicted on similar crimes involving human rights violations and other atrocities.) CODEP reported that the "armed forces responded to the terrorists' crimes with a terrorism infinitely worse than that which they were combatting, since from 24 March 1976 they could operate with the power and impunity of a dictatorship, kidnapping, torturing and murdering thousands of human beings."[8] How and why did state terrorism appear in Argentina?

> In order to guarantee the security of the state, all the necessary people will die.[9]

Three factors combined to produce eight years of state terrorism in Argentina. During that time, no one was safe as the junta rooted out the enemies of the state and the "Argentine way of life."[10] Those three factors included (1) Argentina's ten-year-old struggle with terrorism; (2) Argentina's tradition (shared with many Latin American neighbors) of turning to the military to restore order to the chaotic economy and political situation; and (3) the anticommunist and antiterrorist training and indoctrination that the Argentine military had undergone. These three factors, none unique to Argentina alone, produced the Process of National Reorganization, or what is now known simply as the "dirty war."

1. Argentina's terrorism problem had grown urgent long before the 1976 coup. Founded in 1969 by Roberto Santucho, the *Ejercito Revolucionario del Pueblo* (ERP), the People's Revolutionary Army, modeled itself after the tactics and ideology of Fidel Castro and Ché Guevara. Trying to duplicate Castro's success in Cuba, the ERP operated in rural Argentina, conducting a guerrilla war against the army. The ERP wanted to eliminate capitalism throughout Latin America, beginning in Argentina. The *Montoneros* were also a left-wing organization, one that had split off from the populist-labor Peronist movement. (*Montonero* meant "roughrider," and in nineteenth-century Argentina the *montoneros* or roughriders had struggled with the powerful landowners and ranchers of the pampas.) The *Montoneros* operated primarily in Argentina's cities and came into the spotlight

in 1970 after the kidnapping and murder of General Pedro Eugenio Ahamburu.

Between 1970 and 1973 the *Montoneros* established a reputation for kidnapping and ransoming wealthy Argentines to raise money for the poor. The *Montoneros* became quite popular as a result of their Robin Hood tactics in the early 1970s. By 1975, the year prior to the military coup, the *Montoneros* had begun targeting military and police victims (with murders and bombings), which produced unexpected results. Right-wing death squads, often composed of off-duty policemen, began retaliating against the ERP and *Montoneros*. The Anti-Communist Argentine Alliance (AAA or Triple A) killed over eight hundred suspected left-wing sympathizers in 1975; by March 1976, one political killing occurred every five hours in Argentina and one bomb attack every three hours.[11] The government of Juan Perón's widow, Isabel Perón, could not maintain law and order. The Argentine press and public began calling on the military to step in to restore the peace.

2. Trusting the military to intervene—temporarily—in Argentine politics to restore order and economic prosperity was "standard operating procedure" by 1976. The military had helped consolidate the newly independent state after 1816 and had developed a reputation for discipline and professionalism. As in many other Latin American states, the armed forces were thought to be "above" politics. Military coups in 1930, 1943, 1955, 1962, and 1966 had established a pattern of military intervention to "put things right," and the conditions prevailing in Argentina in 1976 dovetailed with that tradition. Inflation at the beginning of 1976 was running at a projected annual rate of 800 percent, and terrorism from the left and right was rampant. The government of Isabel Perón was ineffectual, and just before she was deposed Perón signed a directive, authorizing the military "to take any action they deemed fit in dealing with terrorism."[12] Many editorials called for emergency action, and all eyes were on Argentina's military leadership to lead the country out of another crisis.

3. The military junta that took power in Argentina in March 1976 had received a type of training and indoctrination unlike any of its predecessors. Schooled in the United States' counterinsurgency programs at Fort Bragg, North Carolina, and in the Panama Canal Zone, over six hundred[13] Argentine officers had been taught how to "extract" information from subversives. Communism was viewed as the enemy of democracy, Christianity, and the Argentine "way of life." The Argentine officers received this training and indoctrination through programs begun under the Kennedy administration (Alliance for Progress), programs that trained the U.S. military to combat communist insurgency in South Vietnam and that prepared the Argentines to fight a dirty war against domestic subversion from the left. Their training had been so thorough that, months before the coup, military

leaders in Argentina had a complete plan for permanently eliminating the ERP, the *Montoneros*, and all subversive sympathizers from Argentina. Their counterinsurgency indoctrination had convinced them that Argentina's terrorism problem required a drastic solution.

The solution that the junta put into operation following the coup of March 1976 had two objectives. First, the subversives and terrorists had to be totally destroyed. Second, the state had to be rid of its enemies without subjecting Argentina to the international criticism and condemnation that Chile had encountered while eliminating subversives under the Pinochet regime. It was not difficult for the junta to identify its targets. All known members and supporters of the ERP and the *Montoneros* were immediately targeted for elimination. But as Army General Videla remarked, a "terrorist is not just someone with a gun or a bomb; he can also be someone who spreads ideas that are contrary to Western and Christian civilization."[14] By 1983, CODEP reported, "subversive" came to include journalists, politicians, labor union activists, priests and nuns, housewives, actors, teachers, students, doctors, lawyers, and armed forces draftees.

Because the junta wanted to preserve Argentina's international reputation, it decided to conduct the "dirty war" against subversives in secret. The hallmark of the dirty war was the method of "disappearing" a suspected subversive. This meant that a suspect would be picked up by one of the many security forces (the army, navy, air force, federal police, city police, the Interior and Foreign Ministries, and the State Information Service all had security forces, each with its own list of suspects); then the suspect would be interrogated, tortured, and killed without any official record of the arrest. There were no arrest warrants on file, and no bureaucrat would acknowledge publicly that the "dirty war" was taking place. Secret jails were set up where interrogations and torture (beatings, electrocution, rape, drowning, burial alive) were conducted. Finally, the corpses were disposed of secretly, either dumped at sea out of airplanes or buried in mass, anonymous graves. Hands and heads often were cut off the corpses to prevent identification. Newspapers were censored, and editors like Jacobo Timerman (*Prisoner without a Name, Cell without a Number*) who denounced the junta's methods were picked up by security forces. The plan was simple: to terrorize the population so thoroughly that no one would speak out against the "dirty war." Immediately following the coup, the government made the following announcement:

> As from April 22, 1976, it is forbidden to report, comment on, or make reference to subjects related to subversive incidents, the appearance of bodies and the deaths of subversive elements and/or members of the armed and security forces, unless these are announced by a high official source. This includes kidnappings and disappearances.[15]

The CODEP report found that the kidnappings, torture, and murders were conducted in nearly identical fashion throughout Argentina by the various security agencies. It concluded that the "dirty war" was an operation run at the highest levels of government but that at least one thousand men helped conduct the kidnappings, torture, and murders. With the press silenced, and the government unwilling to officially acknowledge the "disappearances," fear spread quickly and paralyzed many Argentines. Word of mouth provided the publicity that the news media could not. The terror machine consumed between eleven and thirty thousand victims, destroyed the *Montoneros* and the ERP, and emasculated the Argentine press. The people of Argentina, however, were not without heroes and friends. The silence of the terror and the plan to carry it out in secrecy were first disrupted by mothers whose children had been "disappeared."

Thirteen months after the military coup, on April 13, 1977, fourteen women marched silently on Buenos Aires' Plaza de Mayo. They were protesting the "disappearance" of their children and challenging the official silence imposed by the junta. The "Mothers of the Plaza" knew that they, too, might disappear, and several did over the course of the next several years. They were tear-gassed, harassed, and beaten up by security forces, but every Thursday afternoon they showed up to march and protest in silence. Soon they began to carry photographs of their missing relatives and signs with the victims' names and the dates of their disappearance. The women were joined by sisters, grandmothers, and daughters of Argentines who had disappeared. Then they were joined by sympathetic onlookers. The international media began to cover their story. Meanwhile, the foreign-language press in Argentina and the United States embassy began to assist relatives trying to learn the fate of loved ones. The U.S. embassy began keeping records of all requests for help in tracking down "disappeared" relatives, and soon the massive scope of the "dirty war" began to emerge. President Jimmy Carter was informed of the widespread and systematic violation of human rights in Argentina, and the United States began to pressure the junta to stop the campaign of terror. The Organization of American States sent a commission to Argentina in 1979 to investigate allegations of human rights violations. In 1980, the Nobel Peace Prize was awarded to Adolfo Perez Esquivel in recognition of his work with the Permanent Assembly for Human Rights and of the Service for Peace and Justice. Amnesty International began to investigate the "dirty war." The silence had been broken, but the junta did not step down until after another economic debt crisis and the fiasco of the 1982 Malvinas/Falklands War with Great Britain had discredited military rule. In December 1983, President Raúl Alfonsín was inaugurated, and the following September the National Commission on Disappeared Persons (CODEP) reported its findings to him. Argentina's nightmare was over, but the horror would linger as nearly nine thousand men, women, and children remained missing. The engineers of Argentina's state terrorism have been tried and convicted, but the trauma of the "dirty war" remains.

Soviet Use of Psychiatric Terrorism against Dissidents

State terrorism can be used by governments of the left or right, by states like Argentina fighting communists, or by communist states fighting internal dissidence. Governance by state terror has a long history in the Soviet Union, where it has been refined into a highly specific and technical political weapon. Today, for example, the Soviet state apparatus uses involuntary psychiatric commitment and treatment to terrorize religious and political dissidents. This sophisticated and selective mode of terrorism is the next topic of discussion.

> We live in a society in which no one, including the authors of this letter, can be certain that they will never be . . . inmates of psychiatric hospitals.[16]

The absolute authority and control of the Russian tsars were based on the people's belief that their rulers were divinely appointed. The tsars also used the secret police to root out opposition, backed up by a policy of imprisoning or exiling the politically disaffected. Following the revolutions of 1917, the new communist leaders, beginning with Joseph Stalin, used mass terror to restructure and consolidate the political and social systems of the new USSR. Mass terror, including arrests, deportations, and executions, had several objectives: (1) to preserve and strengthen the Communist Party's dominance; (2) to stifle and punish opposition; (3) to crush organized religion and the last vestiges of local autonomy; (4) to root out individual enterprise; and most important, (5) to create an all-pervading atmosphere of terror and coercion "in which the potential non-conformist hesitated . . . even to speak freely to members of his own family."[17] Mass terror isolated individuals and made the Party the sole, supreme organization through which citizens could act. Stalin, too, used the secret police, NKVD, to watch the general population, as well as the army. In 1930, the GULAG system of prison and labor camps was created by the NKVD to house the victims of Stalin's terror, including millions of peasants and later members of the Party and the military. As the terror proceeded, it became more selective and the numbers diminished, but at its peak Stalin's terror machine caused the arrest of 6 to 10 million Soviets (1935–1936).[18] The mass terror and the purges ended with the onset of World War II, and later were denounced by Stalin's successor, Nikita Khrushchev, in 1956.

In the 1960s, mass terror was replaced by more sophisticated and subtle forms of state terror—political showcase trials and the involuntary hospitalization and treatment of dissidents in psychiatric facilities. The showcase trials of dissidents such as Uli Daniel and Andrei Sinyavsky intimidated other dissidents but also attracted negative publicity from the international community. Reports began leaking out in the late 1960s that the state had undertaken a new, systematic policy of forcibly institutionalizing dissidents in psychiatric hospitals. The switch to psychiatric terror met the government's desire for a "quieter" form of coercion, and it was believed (at the time) that the new technique could alter dissidents' political opinions. Psychiatric hospitalization, at least, might lead to questions about the credibility and sanity of the dissidents. Sometimes dissidents did renounce their criticisms of the government and the policy of psychiatric terror for the most part avoided the intense publicity of the show trials. Two additional factors, however, also contributed to the state's adoption of the policy of compulsory psychiatric hospitalization of dissidents:

1. The imprecise nature of psychiatric diagnosis, and
2. The fact that all psychiatrists practicing in the USSR are state employees.

No normal person can be opposed to the workers' and the peasants' State.[19]

Psychiatry has no objective tests to diagnose mental illness. The criteria psychiatrists use to establish the presence of mental illness consist of cultural and ethical standards of behavior, derived from the society in which psychiatrists practice. Psychiatrists frequently use concepts like "well adjusted to society" to determine mental health, and in a society that values conformity, unconventional behavior (like picketing or requesting an exit visa to Israel) may be considered evidence of mental illness. Psychiatrists like Sidney Bloch have recognized the vulnerability of psychiatry: "The ready labelling of unconventional behavior as socially deviant provides fertile soil for its redefinition as psychiatrically abnormal, a natural foundation on which the use of psychiatry for social repression can take place."[20] The subjective standards by which society—and psychiatrists—measure mental health and illness have produced a situation that can be manipulated to punish deviant or undesirable behavior.

In a system such as the Soviet field of psychiatry and mental health, in which all clinics and hospitals are state-run and all psychiatrists are state employees, the vulnerability of psychiatry to political manipulation has become acute. Soviet dissidents and psychiatrists have reported that some psychiatrists have based their professional success on cooperating with government requests to hospitalize and treat dissidents in psychiatric facilities. Soviet psychiatrist Anatoly Koryagin, himself imprisoned for criticizing Soviet abuses of psychiatry, has documented numerous cases in which "healthy people in the U.S.S.R. are pronounced mentally ill and are condemned to exist as such."[21] Once political patients are brought to psychiatric hospitals by order of the KGB, the Ministry of Internal Affairs or the Procuracy, those individuals are labeled "anti-Soviet" and receive special treatment for their deviant behavior and beliefs. They cannot refuse treatment, and it is professional suicide for another psychiatrist to challenge their diagnosis and treatment.

Involuntary commitment and state-ordered psychiatric terror intimidate the dissident, those who observe the involuntary commitment, and those who hear of it. Koryagin has reported that the government sometimes stages a disturbance (a brawl or quarrel) to justify arrests, sometimes orders dissidents to submit to psychiatric tests, and at other times forcibly removes individuals from their homes without any prior warning. Individuals who have come into conflict with the prevailing order—but otherwise are deemed healthy by their family and friends—find themselves charged with an "anti-Soviet" offense. Confined to a psychiatric ward and declared insane, their confinement is open-ended and indefinite. The treatment is also unpredictable. Some patients have been brutalized, while others have received no clinical treatment whatsoever. Many dissidents have reported that they were ordered by the court to undergo treatment that included insulin coma therapy, electroshock treatment, or narcotherapy. Some dissidents have reported that they were given a choice: recant your views or remain in the hospital. Despite reports that over one thousand people are being held in psychiatric hospitals because of their religious or political views and activities, the use of psychiatry as a weapon against dissidence continues.

In 1974, a Soviet psychiatrist and a dissident, Semyon Gluzman and Vladimir Bukovsky, wrote *A Manual on Psychiatry for Dissenters*. It was a self-published (*samizdat*) underground manual to teach dissidents how to "beat the system" if they were involuntarily hospitalized. Both authors were convicted and imprisoned for "anti-Soviet" behavior as a result of their efforts. The manual is evidence that the community of dissidents in the Soviet Union recognizes the systematic and widespread nature of the state's use of psychiatric terror. Like the Argentines, the Soviet targets of state terror have worked together to resist the government's campaign of fear and have used international publicity to halt the state's attempt to discredit and terrorize dissidents. The American Psychiatric Association (APA) and World Psychiatric Association (WPA) have taken a leading role in publicizing the methods and victims of psychiatric terror. Using tactics employed by Amnesty International, a letter writing campaign to free Dr. Anatoly Koryagin has achieved his release from prison and permission to emigrate.

Summary

The twentieth century has seen an evolution in state terrorism, driven by a heightened sense of state insecurity and fear of rival ideological groups (usually labeled as "outside influences") that criticize or attack the state. Modern state terrorism, like that of Argentina's "dirty war" or the Soviet use of psychiatry to terrorize dissidents, has been made possible by advances in technology (electroshock torture, the use of insulin and other drugs). The Argentine and Soviet cases, however, were also conducted in a manner to avoid what other terrorists seek: the spotlight of international publicity. Argentina and the Soviet Union, nevertheless, have received the attention of international rights organizations (for example, Amnesty International, World Psychiatric Association) seeking to pressure those states to stop terrorizing their own people. The Argentine junta that unleashed the military and police on subversives and suspected subversives was toppled only after the disgrace of the Falklands/Malvinas War with Britain in 1982. The Soviet press, following Mikhail Gorbachev's policy of *glasnost* ("openness") in 1987, began to publish stories of abuses in the psychiatric establishment. These reports followed the release of two dozen dissidents from psychiatric detention in the spring. In 1988, TASS announced that "legal guarantees against possible errors and malpractices" would be instituted to protect patients *and* prevent the commitment of a "patently healthy person." Soviet reforms, like those in Argentina, however, followed international attention and pressure to halt the terror campaigns.

State terrorism is a global phenomenon, confined to no particular ideology or location. The technology of modern terrorism, combined with the manpower of the state's bureaucracy (military, security forces, police, psychiatric staff and facilities), creates a powerful terror machine. Even when trying to operate secretly, state terrorism terrifies and intimidates whole groups, sometimes whole nations, and the remedy to end the terror often must come from external sources. State terrorism represents a small but well-organized and persistent type of terrorism. The international community appears poorly equipped to prevent this form of terrorism, but there have been successes in terminating it when word of the atrocities reaches the outside world.

5
Terrorism and Radical Ideology

Radical or revolutionary ideologies are the third major source of terrorism, after nationalism and state terror. A belief system that calls for deep and rapid political change often invokes terrorism to trigger conflict between the state and the masses to set the process of revolution in motion. Like state terror and struggles for national liberation, radical ideologies that utilize terrorism are not confined to the left or right side of the political spectrum. In this chapter, three examples of terrorism driven by radical ideology are considered: militant Islamic fundamentalism and terrorism; the campaign of terror by West Germany's anarchist-Marxist Baader-Meinhof Gang; and white supremacists in the United States who have conspired to overthrow the U.S. government through assassinations of public officials and other opponents of their beliefs.

Militant Islamic Fundamentalism and Terror

God is our goal, the Prophet is our leader. The Koran is our Constitution, struggle is our way. Death in the service of God is the loftiest of our wishes. God is great, God is great.[1]

To kill and get killed for Allah, That's the message of Ruhollah.[2]

Americans were introduced to the latest revival in Islamic fundamentalism when the U.S. embassy in Tehran, Iran, was occupied in 1979 by students calling themselves "followers of the Imam line" (Khomeini's followers). The tradition that combines Islam and terrorism can be traced back to the Assassins of the eleventh century. The Assassins first appeared in the highlands north of Tehran, led by the charismatic Hasan-i Sabbah. The Assassins were Shi'ite Muslims, and their leader trained his followers as fighters and killers, and used selective murders to terrorize political figures and entire communities. The Assassins believed they were killing the enemies of Islam, and their leader blessed their daggers before their attacks.

The Assassins spread to Syria, and led by the Old Man of the Mountain they terrorized at will until they were crushed by the Mongols in the thirteenth century.

The religious leadership of Shi'ite Muslims in Iran first became involved with terrorism in the 1890s through the *Fedayeen-i Islam*. The "self-sacrificers" or devotees of Islam were led by a Shi'ite theologian and targeted British and Russian officials for assassination. The *Fedayeen* tried to kill the Shah of Iran in 1948, and later backed the Ayatollah Khomeini in his movement to depose the Shah and restore traditional Islamic values to Iran's government and society. Militant Islamic fundamentalism has roots that are older than the Assassins or the *Fedayeen*, however, resting ultimately on the belief that all Muslims have a duty to defend their faith and wage war (*jihad*) on the enemies of Islam. In Iran today, the Ayotollah Khomeini teaches that those enemies include western values, western imperialism, and Israel. Fundamentalists are working to eliminate undesirable western practices (equality of the sexes, drinking, gambling, pornography, etc.), and it is consistent with Shi'ite beliefs to use violence, physical struggles, *jihad*, martyrdom, and even death to combat the enemies of Islam. (Stoning, flogging, and amputation are used to punish domestic crimes.) Militant fundamentalist followers of Khomeini believe the Islamic community is emerging from an era in which alien "infidels" governed them and debased their culture. A violent challenge to western domination deposed the Shah of Iran and helped establish the fundamentalist Islamic government in Tehran today. That government has used terrorism internally to crush dissent (especially from Marxists) and has supported international acts of terrorism by militant fundamentalist Shi'ites. Americans frequently have been the target of radical fundamentalist efforts to destroy the vestiges of western influence, and Islamic fundamentalist terror has killed more Americans than any other type of terrorism.

The new, Islamic constitution of Iran justifies fundamentalist Islamic terrorism. Besides legalizing the authority of the clergy to govern Iran, the constitution of 1979 states that the ideological mission of the army and the Revolutionary Guard includes extending "the sovereignty of God's law throughout the land." Specifically, this translates into a policy of support for groups that use terrorism to protect and promote Shi'ite Islam (particularly in Iraq, Lebanon, and the Persian Gulf states). The course of militant Islamic terrorism since Khomeini consolidated Islamic society and government in Iran has been spectacular.

1981: After crushing the Marxist *mujahedeen* (which had bombed the Islamic Republic Party office in Tehran), the Islamic government executed six thousand *mujahedeen* members and supporters. The new Islamic state then began to look outward. A massive propaganda campaign was directed toward fundamentalists in Malaysia, Pakistan, the Philippines, Turkey, Saudi Arabia, North Yemen, Lebanon, Iraq, Kuwait, and Bahrain.

Thousands of *entaharis* were trained for volunteer suicide attacks against the "enemies of Islam." Camps were set up in Qom and Tehran, with one camp in Tehran reserved for women trainees only.

Anwar Sadat, President of Egypt who made peace with Israel, was assassinated.

1982: After Israel invaded Lebanon, Iran sent hundreds of Revolutionary Guards to the Bekaa Valley to organize and help train fundamentalist Shi'ite guerrillas. Islamic *Jihad*, Islamic *Amal*, *Hezbollah*, and *Al Da'awa* ("The Call") were set up.

1983: The U.S. embassy in Beirut was demolished by a suicide truck bomb (seventeen died).

U.S. Marine Corps barracks near the Beirut Airport was leveled by a suicide truck bomb (241 died); Islamic *Jihad* claimed responsibility for both attacks. (Marines withdrew in February 1984.)

1984: The U.S. embassy annex in a Beirut suburb was bombed. Kidnapping of Americans in Beirut began.

1985: *Hezbollah*, another fundamentalist group, hijacked TWA Flight 847. U.S. Navy Seaman Robert Stethem executed.

1986: CIA station chief in Beirut William Buckley was kidnapped and killed after being tortured by his captors. U.S. arms sales to Iran led to the release of two hostages; kidnappings continued.

1987: Fundamentalist pilgrims incited a riot in Mecca.

Terrorism has proven itself to be an effective instrument for accomplishing the radical goal of driving Westerners and western influence from Iran and parts of Lebanon. Violence, martyrdom, and terrorism have been useful in altering the western and secular orientation of the people there toward the more traditional Islamic lifestyle in which law, economics, politics, and social relations all are based on tenets of the Koran. Most experts doubt whether Iran will be able to carry the revolution far from its borders, but the terrorism it sponsors in Lebanon has created great turmoil there. The Lebanese Shi'ite community is in a stronger position today vis-à-vis other Islamic and Christian sects, but Lebanon lies in ruin. Nonetheless, political terrorism is the legitimate heir to old Shi'ite traditions that blend politics and violence (*jihad*) for revolutionary change. That instrument, honed for centuries, will continue to find employment as the radical reconstruction of Islamic societies continues.

The Baader-Meinhof Gang: Radical Ideology in the Federal Republic of Germany and RAF Terrorism

Terrorism in the Federal Republic of Germany today is not waged to reunite the country (which has been divided since World War II ended), nor is it conducted as part of a religious campaign to restore fundamentalist values to society and government. Terrorism in the FRG is the tool used by radical Marxist-anarchists who hope to spark a popular uprising against the capitalist system of government. What began as student protests in the late 1950s on West German university campuses split into a political movement and a terrorist organization in the 1960s. The ideology of terrorists in the FRG today (much like the ideology of Adolf Hitler) is best identified by what it opposes, what it hates.

West German university students founded the SDS (Socialist Student Union) in 1959 to protest against the authoritarian management of the university system and also against the rearmament of their country as a member of NATO (which included the installation of nuclear weapons in the FRG). Soon their protests expanded to include the Vietnam war, the brutality of the Shah of Iran and the junta in Greece. The students obtained a voice in the running of the universities, but their other protests were in vain. The SDS lost most of its membership by the mid-1960s to the KPD (German Communist Party), which pursued efforts to change West German policies through electoral politics.

Some university and former university students, led by attorney Horst Mahler, founded the *Rote Armee Fraktion*, the Red Army Faction (RAF), to try to change Germany by starting a mass revolution. The RAF, Mahler believed, was to act as a "vanguard" and use the cultural revolution of the 1960s (much of it inspired by the American counterculture) to trigger collective resistance in the FRG against the political establishment. Mahler based the RAF's terrorist tactics on the writings of Brazilian Carlos Marighella (*Manual of the Urban Guerrilla*); Marighella called for terror against the "political machine" through attacks on police stations, judges, politicians, and business corporations. Mahler also drew vaguely on the teachings of Marx, Lenin, Mao, Marcuse, and Bakunin to create an ideology of hatred for capitalism, consumerism, and the United States. Above all else, the RAF hated authority and authority figures and has killed them throughout its struggle to destroy the "Establishment" and bring about "rule by the masses."

In 1968 the RAF began its campaign against bourgeois, consumer society when Andreas Baader and Gudrun Ensslin torched a department store in Frankfurt. The year 1968 proved to be fateful: Rudi Dutschke, leader of the SDS, nearly died in an assassination attempt, and Benno

Ohnesorg, a student anarchist, died after being shot by police during an anti-Shah demonstration. These events radicalized some supporters of the student protest movement, including Ulrike Meinhof, a journalist who covered the trial of Baader and Ensslin that same year. In 1970, Meinhof helped Baader escape from prison, and they rendezvoused in Jordan to train at a PFLP (Popular Front for the Liberation of Palestine) camp. Horst Mahler, meanwhile, was jailed for planning the prison break. Baader and Meinhof took control of the RAF on their return from the Middle East, leading a series of bank robberies and a raid on a NATO arsenal to fund and arm the Red Army Faction. In the tradition of Bonnie and Clyde, the West German media nicknamed the RAF the Baader-Meinhof Gang.

Baader and Meinhof had their busiest year in 1972, when they led the RAF in bombing attacks on police headquarters in Augsberg and Munich, U.S. Army Fifth Corps in Frankfurt, and U.S. headquarters in Heidelberg. The Axel Springer Publishing House was also bombed, completing the target list of police, U.S. military, and corporate "enemies of the revolution." Baader and Meinhof were arrested separately in 1972 after intensive nationwide police searches; they would both eventually die in prison. The RAF began a series of terrorist attacks in 1973 aimed at obtaining the release of their leaders. RAF members joined Black September terrorists in attacking the Saudi Arabian embassy in Khartoum, Sudan. They held diplomats hostage while demanding the release of RAF and *al-Fatah* members held in West German and Israeli prisons. When their demands were rejected, one Belgian and one American diplomat were executed before the embassy crisis ended. The RAF had become a full-blown, international terrorist organization.

In 1974, the RAF members in prison went on hunger strike and Holger Meins died of starvation. (The Holger Meins Commandos claimed responsibility for the assassination of Swedish Prime Minister Olaf Palme in 1986.) The RAF retaliated by assassinating the chief judge of the West Berlin High Court, but their terror tactics did not stop the conviction of Baader, Meinhof, and Ensslin on murder and attempted murder charges. The next year, RAF members continued to carry out terrorist attacks hoping to win the release of their leaders. Political targets were chosen, beginning with the kidnapping of Peter Lorenz, the Christian Democrat party's candidate for mayor of West Berlin. The Bonn government agreed to release six RAF members from prison and to pay $50,000 for Lorenz's release. Hoping next to obtain the release of Baader and Meinhof, the RAF occupied West Germany's embassy in Stockholm. When Bonn refused to make a deal, a shoot-out followed and several embassy officers and RAF members died. In 1975, the RAF continued to cooperate with other "revolutionary groups," joining in the attack on OPEC headquarters in Vienna, Austria. The next year, Baader-Meinhof members assisted in the hijacking of an Air France jet to Entebbe, Uganda, but the RAF would refocus its attention on West German targets after Ulrike Meinhof committed suicide in prison in 1976. After her funeral, which was attended by over four thousand people, the RAF retaliated for what it called Meinhof's "assassination" by bombing U.S. Army headquarters in Frankfurt. In 1977, hoping to obtain Andreas Baader's release, the RAF kidnapped West German industrialist Hans Martin Schleyer. He was killed when the government refused to release Andreas Baader. Next, the RAF hijacked a Lufthansa jet to Mogadishu, Somalia, but the GSG-9 rescue team foiled the hostage situation. In despair, Andreas Baader committed suicide in prison.

Bereft of its leadership, the RAF was quiet in 1978, but in 1979 resumed its "antibourgeois, anti-imperialist, anti-American" campaign by attempting to assassinate the commander of NATO, General Alexander Haig. In 1980, the RAF modified its tactics (if not its overall strategy and ideology) by joining ranks with the antinuclear movement. The West German police by this time had imprisoned most of the RAF, and the West German media had agreed to stop giving the RAF the sensational coverage it had enjoyed from 1972 to 1977. (FRG newspapers had published their manifestos and demands, and television stations had preempted regular programming to provide live coverage of several RAF attacks and hostage crises.) In 1981, the RAF began to emphasize, almost exclusively, NATO and NATO suppliers as its targets of choice. Describing itself as "antimilitarist and anti-imperialist," the Red Army Faction has since carried out numerous attacks on U.S. NATO personnel and facilities in West Germany.

The switch to NATO and primarily American targets has been carried out energetically. (The switch away from German targets also may have led to increased membership in the RAF, as well.) The RAF advertised its new tactics in 1981 using an RPG-7 to attack General Frederick Kroesen, U.S. Army commander in Europe. U.S. facilities in Frankfurt, Ramstein, and Wiesbaden were bombed, and the RAF attempted to bomb a Dow Chemical plant in Dusseldorf and an American library in West Berlin. Again, the West German police cracked down, and numerous arrests quieted the RAF until 1984 when it seemed to reappear like a phoenix from its ashes. Over sixty days, from December 1984 to January 1985, the RAF exploded sixty bombs across Germany, predominantly hitting American targets. By the end of 1985, the RAF had established itself as a serious threat to Americans and NATO forces in the Federal Republic of Germany.

Over forty attacks (bombings, murder) took place that year, including the assassination of a German arms manufacturer who sold weapons to NATO; the U.S. Air Force base at Rhein-Main; and the U.S. Depot at Monchen-Gladbach. The RAF bombed the Frankfurt Airport in a demonstration of its support for *Hezbollah*, which had hijacked TWA Flight 847 to Beirut, and the RAF threatened to attack the Paris air show. Most important, 1985 marked the official declaration of a joint "Political-Military" front[3] in which the RAF would collaborate with the French anarchist group, *Action Direct*, to hit U.S. and NATO targets in Europe. The RAF seems to have taken renewed inspiration from its switch in targets, and NATO forces, especially the American components, have been forced to adopt tighter security measures in response.

The Red Army Faction or Baader-Meinhof Gang is driven by intense ideological hatreds. Characterized by its opposition to authority, capitalism, and militarism, the organization survives despite national police efforts to eradicate it. Psychologists speculate as to the roots of RAF violence; some argue that the spoiled, postwar children of the middle class are having an identity crisis. Other analysts believe the Baader-Meinhof Gang overidentified with the war protest and hippie movements in the United States. Still others believe that the RAF are simply "adventure junkies" rebelling against the orderly, security-conscious West German culture. For the Bonn government and Americans in West Germany, the RAF represents a persistent security threat and remains an ideological curiosity.

The Aryan Nations: Terrorist Ideologies in the United States

On the far right of the American political spectrum, a collection of white-supremacist groups have come together under the umbrella organization of the Aryan Nations. Some profess fundamentalist Christian beliefs, and others display a hatred for state authority reminiscent of the RAF, but the thread tying these groups together is a belief in white racial supremacy and a hatred for the liberal, multiethnic American culture. Like the Islamic fundamentalist movement in Iran and the Baader-Meinhof Gang in Germany, right-wing American radical ideology is based very much in hatred and manifests itself in criminal activity and terrorism. Federal authorities began to take this movement seriously in 1983 when a U.S. district court judge and an FBI agent were the targets of assassination attempts by members of The Order and the Covenant, the Sword and the Arm of the Lord (CSA). Later, the FBI learned that groups in Idaho, Colorado, Michigan, Oregon, Texas, Arkansas, Alabama, Illinois, and Missouri had set up a computer-linked network and were planning to overthrow the government of the United States. Despite their relatively small numbers, right-wing terrorist groups finally were recognized as a serious potential threat to the national security.

Right-wing racist terrorism is not a new phenomenon in the United States. The oldest organization now affiliated with the Aryan Nations is the Ku Klux Klan (KKK), established in 1866 in reaction to the new status of blacks in the South following the Civil War. The KKK, nominally established to "defend" whites, terrorized and murdered blacks with cross-burnings and lynchings. The government banned the KKK during Reconstruction, but it reappeared in 1915 in response to the antiwar (World War I) and women's suffrage movements. The KKK ideology of 1915 consisted of opposition to pacifism, birth control, Jews, blacks, and Roman Catholics. Over the next two decades Darwinism and Marxism joined the list of the KKK's targets, and when the civil rights movement began (marked by the 1954 decision in *Brown v. Board of Education, Topeka, Kansas*), it too was added to the KKK's enemies list. Overt KKK terrorism culminated in August 1964, when the FBI discovered that three civil rights workers had been abducted and murdered near Jackson, Mississippi. Ku Klux Klan members were prosecuted for the murders, which had been intended to intimidate individuals working to register black voters in the South.

In the 1980s the KKK has reappeared and made its presence known primarily through public marches and its support for indebted midwestern farmers fighting eviction from their land. The KKK has participated in the networking efforts of the Aryan Nations, including cross-membership in several organizations.

The Aryan Nations, also known as the Church of Jesus Christ Christian, was established in 1974 in Idaho by Richard Butler. The organization draws together survivalists, tax-resisters, white supremacists, and militant Christian fundamentalists. Butler's group was intensely antisemitic, believing that Jesus Christ was not a Jew and that the United States of America, not Israel, was God's "promised land" for his "chosen" people. The chosen race was exclusively white, and the Aryan Nations supported the idea of setting up a "New Israel" in five northwestern states, a proposal first made by white separatist Robert Miles, former leader of the KKK in Michigan. Richard Butler set up an electronic "bulletin board" enabling right-wing groups to contact each other. Evidence of conspiracy among those groups to topple the government, establish guerrilla training camps, destroy utility plants, contaminate water supplies, counterfeit U.S. currency, provide false identities, and carry out armed robberies to finance these efforts has been uncovered by the FBI's investigations. In April 1987, fifteen members of these organizations were indicted on charges of seditious conspiracy or in connection with the 1984 murder of Denver radio disc jocky Alan Berg. (Berg, who was Jewish, had mocked the white supremacist groups on his radio talk show. He was killed with a submachine gun on the streets of Denver on June 18, 1984.)

Like the RAF, other right-wing American groups have acquired a paramilitary terrorist reputation. The Order, a neo-Nazi, white supremacist organization, is thought to be responsible for bombings and multimillion dollar robberies of Brink's trucks. To become a member, an "Aryan Warrior" of The Order, it has been reported that a candidate must kill a Jew, a liberal, a black, or a federal agent or judge. (The April 1987 indictments included five charges of conspiracy to murder a U.S. district judge and an FBI agent.)

Posse Comitatus has also established a reputation for armed conflict with federal authorities and considers the U.S. government to be the "synagogue of Satan." Posse Comitatus ideology blends Christian fundamentalism with white supremacy and a militant individualism that expresses itself in tax evasion. Posse Comitatus followers (typically white, raised in rural, fundamentalist families, self-employed, high school drop-outs, and gun owners) believe that Anglo-Saxons, not Jews, are the true descendants of Abraham. They distrust bankers and lawyers, and believe a man's land is sacred, so sacred that he can defend it against trespassers with deadly force, if necessary. The two most famous members of Posse Comitatus, Gordon Kahl and Arthur Kirk, both died in blazing gun battles with law enforcement officers. Gordon Kahl, a tax evader, held in contempt all gun laws, speed laws, hunting laws, and state and federal taxes. He was accused of murdering two federal marshalls when he died in a gun battle in Arkansas after a cross-country manhunt. Arthur Kirk was an overextended, indebted Nebraska farmer facing foreclosure when he found help from Posse Comitatus. Believing his farm failure to be the result of a "conspiracy" between "Jewish bankers and lawyers," Kirk adopted the Posse Comitatus belief that a man's "land is sacred." Kirk died in a shoot-out with the Nebraska State Patrol in 1984 after he had shot at sheriffs trying to evict him from his farm.

The motley, violent assortment of groups collectively known as right-wing white supremacists are found across the United States. Their numbers remain small, but their paramilitary expertise and willingness to use terrorism have made them a threat that federal authorities no longer ignore. Along with ideologically motivated abortion clinic bombers, the Aryan Nations were responsible for fifteen bombings and 149 attempted bombings in 1986. Terrorist bombings tripled from 1985 to 1986 and caused $3.4 million in damage. Right-wing terrorism against people and property in the United States, committed to overthrowing the government, has been a much smaller threat than the terrorism carried out by the RAF or Islamic fundamentalists. In the context of the American political milieu, however, which tends to be nonideological and committed to compromise, right-wing ideological terrorism is all the more frightening in its fury and fanaticism.

Summary

Radical ideological groups constitute the third major source of terrorism. Radical groups employ terrorism hoping to trigger sudden and deep political change, and are not confined to left or right-wing beliefs or by geography. Two characteristics unite radical terrorist groups: their willingness to use violence and their deep opposition to the status quo. In the Federal Republic of Germany, for example, the left-wing anarcho-Marxist Red Army Faction uses terrorism against a capitalist state that is a key member of NATO. In Iran, Islamic fundamentalists support terrorism to reverse the influence of Western secular values within that country and abroad. In the United States, right-wing racist groups use terrorism to combat a liberal culture and state authority, with particular emphasis given to blacks, Jews, the FBI, and police. Radical ideological groups often resort to terrorism when their critique of the status quo is ignored or frustrated. Like nationalist groups that also use terrorism, radical ideological groups are driven by powerful ideas and ideals that are more difficult to combat than the groups themselves, and tend to survive the immediate membership of the radical groups promoting them.

6
Media Coverage and Terrorism

> Violence and propaganda have much in common. Violence aims at behavior modification by coercion. Propaganda aims at the same by persuasion. Terrorism is a combination of the two.
> —Alex Schmid and Janny deGraaf, *Violence as Communication* (1982), p. 14

Publicity is an integral part of terrorism, and the news industry is a primary conduit connecting terrorists, the public, and governments. Terrorism poses new problems and difficult choices for societies that have popularly elected leadership and respect the freedom of the news media. This chapter will consider three questions:

1. What is the role of publicity in terrorism?
2. Is censorship the answer to the terrorist publicity problem?
3. How have liberal democratic states managed the problem of terrorist publicity?

Anarchists of the nineteenth century hoped to use press coverage of bombings and assassinations to stir up public support and make governments appear incompetent and impotent. "Propaganda by the Deed" was designed to exploit newspapers (and their audience's) appetite for new stories that were violent, emotional, or sensational. Publicity served many purposes: to attract new recruits for the cause; to persuade the public that the government could not protect them; to frighten the leadership, perhaps into using unpopular antiterrorism measures; and ultimately, to provoke disorder and revolution. Although not successful in all the goals of "Propaganda by the Deed," the anarchists taught a very important lesson to their successors: the news can be an unintentional friend to terrorism. Modern terrorists have continued this train of thought, exploiting a news industry that now includes not only the press but also radio and television, as well as international news agencies that feed stories to the local news industry. The electronic media can reach a vast audience almost instantaneously, and satellites make live coverage possible almost anywhere in the world.

Publicity and Terrorism

Publicizing terrorist attacks, especially hostage-taking incidents in which the captors hold press conferences, gives terrorists a platform to address a wide audience. From that platform terrorists can promote their cause, air their grievances, curry sympathy, and recruit new followers. (News coverage is sometimes so graphic and powerful that it inspires imitations.) During the 1972 Olympic Games in Munich, the kidnappers of Israeli athletes had a global audience of perhaps 800 million viewers[1] who were introduced to the desperation and grievances of the Palestinians. Many had never before heard of the Palestinians or their complaints against the state of Israel. The "Black September" terrorists successfully diverted media coverage of the games to their cause, and showed how valuable such publicity could be for communicating with a worldwide audience. There were many benefits. Europeans received further exposure to the Israeli-Palestinian dispute, but a shift in public policy more sympathetic to the Palestinians only came with the Yom Kippur War one year later and the oil embargo that followed it (imposed by OAPEC, the Organization of Arab Petroleum Exporting Countries, to punish the friends of Israel for resupplying the depleted Israeli war stocks). Publicity of the Palestinian "Black September" group's use of terrorism further contributed to existing contacts and "networking" between European and Middle Eastern terrorist groups. Media coverage made groups aware of one another (if they weren't already) and helped them "find" each other more easily than might have been the case without so much publicity. Groups that had been protesting the Vietnam war (such as the German Red Army Faction) found a new focus or cause, while many west European governments shifted their foreign policies to a more pro-Palestinian position. (The shift followed the "oil shock" of the 1973–1974 embargo but was also consistent with public opinion.)

In the United States, terrorist groups have also used media coverage to publicize their demands. The Symbionese Liberation Army (SLA) in 1974 kidnapped Patricia Hearst, whose father Randolph Hearst owned the *San Francisco Examiner*, among many other media investments. The kidnappers demanded a food "giveaway" (paid for out of the Hearst family fortune) and accompanying media coverage. Unfortunately for the group, Patty Hearst became the "media star" while the SLA played a secondary role until tracked down by the police and eliminated in a fiery shoot-out. The terrorist episode attracting the greatest media coverage and making the most powerful impression on the American public was the 1979–1981 occupation of the U.S. embassy in Tehran and the detention of fifty-four Americans. This episode was not meant to gain followers for the group occupying the embassy. The publicity attending these events was used to communicate the terrorists' opposition to the American decision to admit the Shah of Iran to the United States for "medical" reasons. The terrorists also publicized their demand that the Shah be returned to Iran (in exchange for the American hostages) to face prosecution by the new government led by the Ayatollah Khomeini. The intense media coverage surrounding the Americans held hostage gave the Iranian captors a platform from which to publicize their grievances and make their demands. That platform enabled them to speak to the American public in an attempt to manipulate popular opinion and put pressure on the U.S. government to "give up" the Shah.

Two characteristics of the western media are particularly useful to terrorists: news media competition and "sensationalism." These features enable terrorists to use the free media as a platform for propaganda and recruitment. Competitiveness in the news industry and the urgent need to "break" a story first or the pressure to get a scoop before other reporters work to produce an emphasis on "headline" news. Live video coverage or on-the-scene interviews dominate news stories of terrorist crises. The chaotic image of reporters trampling each other to cover the Beirut press conference held by the skyjackers of TWA Flight 847 in June 1985 remains an uncomfortable memory. The pressure to report often provides terrorists with an uncritical platform, an open stage. Whatever the terrorist does or wishes to say is reportedly directly, unedited, to the public. The propaganda potential of this arrangement is tremendous and frequently exploited.

The sensationalism that surrounds terrorism and the news media coverage it receives is also a device manipulated by terrorists. Bombings, skyjackings, and kidnappings contain all the necessary elements to attract media attention: horror, excitement, and violence. The media and their audience seem to have an appetite for "new" news and sensational news. Fifty thousand deaths on American highways are shocking but old news. A bomb explosion in Beirut is unexceptional, but an explosion on the Champs Elysees in Paris or at a Berlin discotheque patronized by U.S. servicemen will get immediate attention. As one Palestinian summarized the problem of getting attention, "We would throw roses if it would work."[2] Other critics have accused the news media of playing to the public's emotions instead of presenting the difficult and complex stories that provide the backdrop to the resort to sensational violence. Concern about terrorist manipulation of a free and competitive news industry is widespread. Many public opinion polls reflect this:

Gallup Poll (USA) October 1986[3]

i. Press coverage gives terrorists
   —too much coverage: 51%
   —too little coverage: 7%
   —right amount of coverage: 40%
ii. Press coverage increases chances
   of future terrorist acts: 60%
   Press coverage reduces chances of
   future terrorist acts: 7%
iii. Terrorists' manipulation of the
   press is a major factor in poor
   press coverage of terrorists incidents (agreed): 52%

Law enforcement officials and media heads differ in their concern over terrorist manipulation of the news media. A fundamental disagreement emerged between law enforcement and news officials when asked, "Do you believe live television coverage of terrorist acts encourages terrorism?"

Ninety-three percent of police chiefs believed that television coverage encourages terrorism, but only 43 percent of newpaper editors and 35 percent of television new directors agreed with that argument.[4]

The sometimes sensational and uncritical coverage provided to terrorists is blamed for many related problems. Unrestricted coverage of hostage-taking episodes has been known to provide terrorists with valuable information about police tactics. For example, the *Hanafi* Muslims who seized 134 hostages in Washington, D.C., in 1977 were told about police snipers by reporters. Terrorism coverage is often blamed for "copycat" imitations as well as unofficial reprisals that follow terrorist episodes (Arabs and Iranians were harassed and beaten up on U.S. streets and campuses after the Tehran embassy was seized in 1979 and again in 1985 when TWA Flight 847 was skyjacked to Beirut and U.S. Navy Seaman Robert Stethem was murdered.)

Media coverage gives terrorists many things they want:

Attention,

A huge audience,

An opportunity to make public their grievances and demands,

A chance to recruit new members and increase their popular support,

An occasion to make the government appear impotent if it negotiates or harsh and repressive if it cracks down on terrorists,

An opportunity to demonstrate that law enforcement and the state cannot protect the public.

George F. Will, a newspaper columnist and television commentator, criticizes the news industry for rewarding terrorists with more coverage as their attacks become more violent and outrageous. Will has called television "an electronic megaphone"[5] for terrorists. By allowing themselves to become a conduit between terrorists and the public, the news media appear to play into the terrorists' hands. This has led to many calls for censorship, even by journalists themselves, including Charles Krauthammer:

> Journalists must recognize that there exists a unique class of political events, media terrorism; these acts acquire importance by, and often are undertaken with the sole intention of, being broadcast over the media. Because of the symbiotic relationship between the media and terrorist acts, because these acts are created or at least greatly amplified by media coverage, journalists must exercise self-restraint—call it censorship if you like.[6]

The news media and terrorists find themselves caught in an upward spiral: terrorist violence must be increasingly spectacular to attract the media's and the public's attention. To intervene in this process and halt the upward spiraling of violence and media attention, there are increasing calls for self-restraint, news blackouts by law enforcement or censorship in reporting on terrorism.

Is Censorship the Answer to the Terrorist Publicity Problem?

Self-restraint is not a virtue that the media industry necessarily respects or rewards. Because of the unrestrained pursuit of information during terrorist episodes, some experts think the media risk replacing police or diplomatic negotiators in terrorist crises. Some experts believe media coverage increases the danger to hostages. During those crises, the competing (and sometimes conflicting) interests of the media and government can be seen: the media pursue information, the government seeks order and resolution of the crisis. Both sides believe they are acting in the public's interest. Supporters of an independent news industry believe that only an informed public can govern itself and make democracy work. The very first amendment to the United States Constitution established the rights of a free press and freedom of speech, and the news industry argues that any infringement of those freedoms undermines democracy. Because the public relies on and trusts an independent news industry to keep it informed, censoring the coverage of terrorist events would undermine the public's confidence in the news media. Some censorship would set a precedent for more censorship; in no time the public would lose faith in the media and would be deprived of the data needed to make informed and thoughtful decisions. According to this argument, a news industry free of government control and censorship is a prerequisite for informed public opinion, the backstop of a democracy. Terrorism highlights the tension between a "free press" and a democratic government, however. Facing a hostage-taking episode, the pressure on the government to censor the news becomes intense. Balanced against the public's right to know is government's need to deal secretly and swiftly with terrorists to settle a crisis. The pressure of media coverage on democratic governments trying to resolve terrorist situations has produced an ongoing dialogue between law enforcement and news media personnel. That dialogue has produced two developments in the terrorism-publicity debate: a detailed list of arguments against censorship and media guidelines for the coverage of terrorism.

Terrorism is like a cancer, according to Morton Dean, CBS political reporter, but the appropriate way to fight it is to direct public attention to it, "even if that glare of attention makes some people and some governments feel uncomfortable."[7] Eight arguments against censoring news coverage of terrorism appear, in one form or another, in most discussions about the terrorist publicity problem:

1. To understand a problem and make careful policy choices, the public must be informed. If the public gives up its right to know, it gives up the right to self-government.

2. Any censorship will undermine the news media's credibility.

3. Censorship of reporting on terrorism lulls the public into believing it is safe and that there is no terrorist threat. This ignorance undermines the public's ability to comprehend and respond to terrorism effectively when it does occur.

4. The rumor mill is more sensationalistic and inaccurate than a free news media. Rumors about terrorism can create panic and hysteria out of proportion to the threat, causing further problems for law enforcement officials trying to resolve a terrorist crisis.

5. Terrorists will do whatever is necessary to attract public attention. Censorship might cause more outrageous acts than those presently committed by terrorists and covered by the media.

6. Censorship might encourage government or law enforcement officials to take action that the public would not approve. Media coverage holds them to a high standard of behavior and discourages the use of tactics that violate human and civil rights.

7. Censorship would be a victory for terrorists who want to force the state to take undemocratic and repressive measures. Those measures undermine democratic principles and popular support for the government.

8. Censorship of news coverage of terrorism indicates that a government is treating symptoms (violence, publicity) rather than attacking

the causes of terrorism. Political terrorists do not seek publicity for its own sake but rather to accomplish certain goals. A government policy focusing on publicity and censorship may signal a failure to grasp the nature of the problems giving rise to terrorism.

Although the news industry has vigorously defended free speech, it has also begun to scrutinize how it covers terrorism and how it may have been manipulated. The major American television networks, major newspapers, and international news agencies have prepared (and continue to revise) guidelines for editors and reporters covering terrorism. Columbia Broadcasting System (CBS) has written guidelines for the coverage of terrorism on network television. Those guidelines include the following advice:

1. Encourage denying terrorists live video coverage.
2. Advise reporters not to interfere with police handling of terrorist attacks.
3. Recommend that reporters consult authorities on inflammatory language that should not be employed.
4. Counsel balanced coverage of all terrorist activities.[8]

The other networks, international news agencies like United Press International (UPI), and most large newspapers now have internal guidelines for covering terrorism stories. Those guidelines indicate that the news industry is indeed aware of the risk of manipulation by terrorists and the danger of romanticizing their actions, as well as the need to cooperate with law enforcement (or at least avoid interfering with the resolution of a terrorist episode). In practice, however, the intense competition for a story still produces unedited coverage (e.g., the Beirut Airport press conference held by the skyjackers of TWA Flight 847 in June 1985) and headline coverage giving terrorists the spotlight they desire. As a conduit from terrorists to the public, the news industry finds itself confronting a dilemma: how to inform the public about terrorism without becoming a propaganda machine for the terrorists. As a conduit from the public to government by way of editorial commentary, the news industry confronts another dilemma: how to maintain an editorial position that opposes terrorism while, for example, covering human interest stories in which public pressure to get hostages released is always intense.

Terrorism creates other problems for the news industry of democratic states in addition to propaganda and censorship. Those problems include news blackouts and misinformation, problems that the news media have experienced while covering terrorism in the United Kingdom, the Federal Republic of Germany, and the United States.

Liberal Democratic States and the Terrorist Publicity Problem: The United Kingdom, West Germany, and the United States

United Kingdom

The United Kingdom's long-standing problem in Northern Ireland with the terrorism that stems from the division of Ireland has led to government efforts to "manage" news coverage of political violence in that area. Since "the troubles" grew more serious in the late 1960s and early 1970s, the U.K. government has employed news blackouts and censorship to affect the content and tone of news coverage of terrorism in Northern Ireland. The government's task has been made easier due to state ownership of British Broadcasting Corporation (BBC) radio and television. Independent television and the press, however, have also come under government pressure not to publicize terrorism and not to criticize government policy regarding terrorism.

BBC journalists (like those at CBS) have a set of guidelines to follow when reporting stories about Northern Ireland or the Irish Republican Army (IRA). BBC journalists must clear their stories through several levels of editors and management staff. The result: many stories are not covered at all; or the reporters "self-censor"—i.e., they do not pursue stories they expect will be rejected by BBC management. In 1985, BBC television reporters and staff around the world staged a twenty-four-hour work stoppage to protest a decision by the BBC board of governors not to broadcast a documentary prepared by BBC staff. Entitled "Northern Ireland: At the Edge of the Union," the documentary looked at the current situation in Northern Ireland and interviewed leaders from Protestant/royalist and Catholic/republican organizations. Because the Catholic spokesman was alleged by authorities to belong to the IRA, the British government requested that the BBC deny him a platform from which to address the public. (Rule 3 of the BBC *News Guide* states, "The IRA must not be interviewed without prior authority . . . ") Because of the uproar, the BBC board of governors decided to broadcast a slightly edited version of the documentary, which later aired in the United States in the autumn of 1985. (The BBC has had several other programs banned or edited, including "24 hours" [1971]; "The Scottish Connection" [1976]; "The City on the Border" [1978]; and "A Bridge of Sorts" [1978].)

The British government does not have similar leverage in a formal sense with independent television companies in Britain. In the past, however, authorities overseeing independent television coverage have met with government and law enforcement officials from Northern Ireland and agreed informally to omit news stories on the IRA. The result: independent and BBC television coverage of terrorism in Northern Ireland has been incomplete. A study by British journalists concluded that the results of government management of the news have been twofold:

1. The public does not understand the violence in Northern Ireland, and
2. The public does not trust the press to accurately and critically report news of terrorism originating in Northern Ireland's troubles.[9]

The British tradition of restraining the news media when stories involve "national security" is hardly a new phenomenon. "D-notices" (defense notices) have been issued to newspaper editors to prevent publicity of "national security" matters, a practice dating back to World War II but still in use in the 1980s. Scotland Yard continues to embargo information on investigations into terrorist bombings and kidnappings, and British newspapers have proven to be the most cooperative medium in maintaining news blackouts. Overall, the government and law enforcement have been successful in managing news coverage of terrorism despite a British tradition of aggressive and competitive journalism. British journalists, however, recognize that "managing the news" can extract a high price in media credibility and public understanding of the complex issues terrorism presents to democratic societies.

The Federal Republic of Germany

The United Kingdom has had decades of experience dealing with political problems, terrorism, and news management in Northern Ireland. The Federal Republic of Germany did not have the benefit of long experience when terrorism made a dramatic entrance into German politics in 1972. The Olympic Games held in Munich that year brought home the lesson of how powerful an instrument the news media—particularly international television—can be in a terrorist campaign. Following the tragic resolution of Black September's attack on Israeli athletes (all the hostages died in a rescue attempt), the West German state confronted a stepped-up campaign of bombings and kidnappings by the Baader-Meinhof Gang, officially the Red Army Faction (RAF). The RAF had become active in the late 1960s protesting capitalism, imperialism, and the Vietnam war in a series of bombings. After the Munich attack the group shifted its tactics to emphasize kidnappings, which provided a better opportunity to demand that their communiqués be published in the press and read over radio and television.

In 1974 the RAF kidnapped Peter Lorenz, leader of the Christian

Democratic Party of West Berlin, and several communiqués were publicized. By 1977, however, when the RAF struck again and kidnapped industrialist Hans Martin Schleyer, the news media and the government already had reached an understanding on the terrorism publicity problem. The government's strategy was twofold: to work with the media to deny the RAF access to print and airwave publicity; and to coordinate the news coverage that did reach the public.

The strategy elicited extraordinary cooperation from the West German news industry. Despite over a hundred RAF messages and communiqués, almost no terrorist communications demanding the release of RAF prisoners were published. The media did agree to publish false reports of government efforts to arrange the release of terrorists whose freedom the RAF had demanded in exchange for Schleyer's life. For nearly two months the terrorists were denied a public platform, and the German people quietly accepted the news blackout. Schleyer died before he could be rescued, but the attempt to manage news coverage was a success.

This type of government media cooperation reappeared late in 1986 when German security forces captured Lebanese terrorists believed to be responsible for skyjacking an American jet to Beirut in 1985. When the U.S. government announced its intention to seek extradition of those individuals, two West German citizens were kidnapped in Beirut. The kidnappers demanded an exchange of prisoners in order to prevent the extradition of the Lebanese to the United States from the FRG. To limit publicity and pressure on German leaders, the government again "blacked out" news reports on extradition proceedings, and the West German news media cooperated in silence. The West German government was able to negotiate quietly, free of publicity and public demands for updates. American journalists remember the last case of such cooperation between the government and American journalists was during World War II when the press corps worked closely and reliably with the military command. The American news industry is amazed at the West German management of the news and somewhat uneasy about it.

The United States

The American news industry is not subject to the controls that the BBC must respect in the United Kingdom, nor do American journalists demonstrate the respect for authority that the West German media display when reporting on terrorism. The American news industry often adopts an adversarial role vis-à-vis the government (as watchdog), and there is intense competition within the industry to break stories. As a result, cooperative news blackouts are uncommon in terrorist crises involving Americans. In domestic terrorist coverage (the Weather Underground, Black Panthers, Ku Klux Klan, abortion clinic bombings) or when covering terrorism outside the United States' borders (Marine Corps barracks bombing [1983], *Achille Lauro* attack ([1986]), the U.S. news industry rarely encounters government censorship or self-censorship. Investigative reporting is too powerful a tradition for the U.S. government to restrain; therefore, it has adopted different tactics in dealing with the terrorist publicity problem.

Two major hostage-terrorism problems, the 1979–1981 occupation of the U.S. embassy in Tehran and the multiple kidnappings of Americans in Beirut (following the Israeli incursion in 1982) led the Carter and Reagan administrations to adopt new techniques for dealing with the terrorist publicity problem. Rather than using censorship or news blackouts, the administrations employed misdirection and disinformation techniques to ease the burdens of publicity and public pressure during the hostage situations. Prior to the failed rescue mission of April 1980, the Carter administration repeatedly stated its commitment to negotiating the hostages' release and the president's rejection of any violent measures that might endanger the safety of the fifty-four Americans being held in Tehran. While the denials took place and the administration negotiated with Iran, a rescue mission was planned and carried out (unsuccessfully). Similarly, the Reagan administration was publicly committed to a policy of "no deals with terrorists," while it secretly shipped weapons and spare parts to Iran in exchange for the release of Americans held by pro-Iranian Shi'ite groups in Beirut. The "misdirection" of public and media attention per se was not denounced on either occasion, but the Reagan administration's disinformation campaign in the summer and fall of 1986 did provoke a hostile reaction from the news media. Following the U.S. attack on Libya in April 1986, the administration intentionally began leaking false rumors of further reprisals against the Kaddafi regime for its sponsorship of international terrorism. The leaks were intended to frighten Kaddafi and to capitalize further on the earlier raid. Realizing that it had been used in a disinformation scheme and fearing its credibility had been undermined, the news industry published all available details on the disinformation campaign.

The U.S. government has not tried to impose censorship on the American news industry, although subtler attempts have been made to "manage" the coverage of terrorist crises. The rigor of the industry and the tradition of a vocal and critical press inhibit any attempts at outright censorship. Intense coverage of Americans held hostage and publicity campaigns by their families did put great pressures on the presidents to obtain the release of captive Americans. Both presidents pursued strategies that failed, although neither Carter nor Reagan blamed the media for forcing him to choose between individual Americans and a national security policy not to deal with terrorists.

Summary

Democratic states with independent news media are learning to appreciate the complex role that publicity and the news industry play in terrorism. The media connect the terrorist to the public, the public to the government, and have also served as a conduit (of disinformation) from states to terrorists. Democratic states confront the thorny dilemma of trying to deny terrorists a platform without undermining civil liberties, especially freedom of speech. The experiences of the United Kingdom, the Federal Republic of Germany, and the United States indicate that the learning process continues, and the search goes on for a way to deny terrorists—but not the public—the benefits of a free news media.

7

The Superpowers, Foreign Policy, and Terrorism

Terrorism is a flexible, highly adaptable political instrument. Its usefulness in nationalist struggles for autonomy or liberation is well known and frequently employed. Increasingly, terrorism is used to promote the ideas and objectives of radical ideologies while governance by terror continues on the left and right of the political spectrum. Terrorism also has become an instrument of foreign policy since World War II, particularly important, some claim, to the repertoire of the two superpowers. Since 1945, the international political environment has been changed by three developments that have elevated the use and importance of terrorism, particularly for the Soviet Union and the United States.

1. World War II ended with many of the old, great powers left prostrate. Germany, France, and Great Britain saw world politics lose its Eurocentric focus; the US-USSR relationship took center stage, and the two new "super" powers began a long-term ideological rivalry.

2. The Soviet-American rivalry, with its strong ideological underpinnings, had to manifest itself in an age of nuclear weapons. The United States ended its war with Japan by detonating nuclear devices over Hiroshima and Nagasaki in 1945. Four years later, the USSR successfully detonated its first atomic bomb, ushering in the age of apocalyptic warfare. The destructive power of nuclear weapons now provides the two superpowers with the capability of destroying most life on the planet. Consequently, the United States and Soviet Union have sought to compete in ways more indirect and with lower risks. To avoid a direct conflict and the exchange of nuclear firepower that might escalate into a global holocaust, the United States and USSR carry out an arms race and arms control talks, conduct clandestine activities and covert operations, act through proxies, and sponsor and engage in terrorism to promote their interests. These activities are less costly and less risky than direct conflict; most are also deniable.

3. With the emergence of the Third World (Latin America, Africa, the Middle East, and Asia) as the focus of Soviet-American rivalry, terrorism came into its own as an instrument of foreign policy. The European theater

had come to hold too high a risk for costly conflict. The large Red Army presence and the American nuclear umbrella offsetting it, together with NATO and Warsaw Pact forces poised along the Iron Curtain, have made Europe an extremely dangerous site for open U.S.-Soviet conflict. At the same time, the war that left the great European powers incapacitated after World War II also weakened their grasp on their colonies. In the Middle East, Africa, and Asia, irregular and unconventional resistance against colonial powers increased; guerrilla warfare and terrorism became popular weapons in many struggles for independence. The presence of indigenous groups using terrorism to achieve political goals provided an opportunity for the Superpower rivalry to express itself in and through many organizations and conflicts in the Third World.

The Superpower-terrorism "connection" assumes many forms. It may take the form of support for groups using terrorism against friends or allies of the rival superpower, or against that superpower directly. "Support" includes providing funds, weapons, training, political endorsement or other logistical assistance (passports, intelligence, use of diplomatic facilities, etc.) to groups that use terrorism. The support may be channeled through a proxy or delivered directly by the superpowers' own military and intelligence services. Cuba frequently is identified by the United States as a Soviet proxy in Latin America and Africa, while expatriate Cubans in the nationalist-terrorist group known as Omega 7 are considered American proxies due to attacks on Chilean and Cuban officials. U.S. aid to Afghani *mujahedeen* resisting Soviet occupation and Soviet support of Palestinian efforts against what they consider Israeli occupation of Palestinian lands are further examples of the indirect Soviet-American conflict that often involves terrorism, proxies and allies. Neither superpower officially admits to sponsoring terrorism or publicly endorses terrorism, and the evidence to substantiate their involvement is scarce, indirect, or frequently unavailable. Given the "plausible deniability" that attends superpower involvement with terrorism, the following two sections address the diverse schools of thought on terrorism and foreign policy. Ranging from denial to international conspiracy networks, this area is perhaps the most speculative of all approaches to international terrorism.

Soviet Foreign Policy and Terrorism

In the 1970's terrorism, whether backed directly or indirectly by the Soviet Union or independently initiated, appeared to have become an indispensable tactical and strategic tool in the Soviet struggles for power and influence within and among nations. In relying on this instrument, Moscow seems to aim in the 1980's at achieving strategic ends in circum stances where the use of conventional armed force is deemed inappropriate, ineffective, too risky or too difficult.[1]

Karl Marx believed that a proletarian culture inevitably would displace the international system that consisted of states and capitalism. His heirs, disappointed by the success that states had enjoyed in getting workers to fight in World War I, were receptive to Lenin's argument that revolutions must be made to happen. Lenin believed that successful revolutions consisted of concerted effort and controlled violence. Terrorism, as long as it was part of an organized scheme and controlled from above, was an acceptable tactic in the revolutionary struggle. After the second Russian revolution in 1917 and Bolshevik victory, training camps were set up in Tashkent as part of the Third International effort to assist colonies struggling for independence. Lenin believed that the struggle against capitalism would be a global revolutionary effort, and the training in Tashkent included military, agitation, and propaganda techniques.

Lenin died in 1924, and the leading advocate of international revolution, Trotsky, lost his role in the new Soviet leadership. Joseph Stalin consolidated power and pursued a strategy known as "socialism in one country." Stalin concentrated on modernizing and industrializing the new Soviet state and was less inclined to support revolutionary and terrorist groups outside the USSR. Soviet foreign policy did target western labor unions for infiltration and governments for subversion. Most energies were directed inward, however, and would remain so until Stalin died in 1953. Nikita Khrushchev, who consolidated his control of the Party and government in 1956, set Soviet foreign policy on a new path. Seeking to avoid direct, cataclysmic conflict with the United States, Khrushchev opened the era of "peaceful coexistence" by shifting Soviet emphasis away from the West and toward the Third World. There, old colonial empires were disintegrating and national wars of liberation were erupting. Supporting revolutionary groups in their efforts to end Western colonial domination offered a low-cost, low-risk chance to expand Soviet influence. There was no need to commit Soviet troops, but weapons, training, intelligence, and money were made available. Clandestine aid to Algerian terrorist groups in 1958 established that the strategy would work, and Khrushchev's shift toward supporting revolutions in the Third World remains a cornerstone of Soviet foreign policy today.

Since 1964 and the advent of the Brezhnev administration, two developments have modified Khrushchev's strategy of supporting revolutionary and terrorist groups. (1) Czechoslovakian General Jan Sejna, an expert in military intelligence who defected to the West in 1968, reported that the KGB played a leading role in the new Soviet foreign policy and that the Politburo had greatly increased the amount of money it committed to supporting Third World revolutions. (2) With the success of Fidel Castro in Cuba, the relentless determination of the Vietnamese resistance and the formation of a Palestinian umbrella organization (PLO), the Soviet Union was assured it would have revolutionary contacts in Latin America, the

Middle East, and Asia. (Cuban troops would enter the Angolan conflict in Africa in 1975.)

Soviet Foreign Minister Alexei Kosygin spoke of "the right of peoples, arms in hand, to oppose aggression or to strive for national liberation"[2] in 1972 in a speech that stressed the importance of avoiding conflict with the United States. (The Vietnam war and the Egyptian-Israeli border situation were quite tense at that time.) While striving to avoid a head-on conflict with the United States, the Soviets began arming the PFLP, training other Palestinians in Havana, and establishing weapons and explosives schools in Czechoslovakia and East Germany. When the Israeli Defense Forces (IDF) briefly occupied parts of Lebanon south of the Litani River in 1978, they discovered maps in Russian and certificates naming Palestinian graduates of the Soviet Ministry of Defense Command and Staff College programs.[3] (Soviet weapons were also discovered in numerous Palestinian strongholds.) The Soviet Union does not deny it supports revolutionary groups, but it does reject the labeling of their tactics as "terrorist." The Western view of the Soviets' foreign policy supporting revolutionary groups is split into two schools of thought. The "international terrorist network," as it has come to be known, is the more radical, conspiratorial view of Soviet foreign policy and terrorism; Soviet "opportunism" is the alternate approach to Soviet involvement with international terrorism. Both groups interestingly refer to much the same body of evidence to support their claims.

The "international terrorist network" is a theory that most international terrorism is organized, funded, armed, supported, and directed by the Soviets to weaken the Western democracies without risking nuclear war (see figure 7–1). The "international terror network" is looked on as one part of a broader Soviet campaign that also includes disinformation, espionage, subversion, and the phony "peace offensive," all intended to undermine the Soviets' enemies. Journalist Claire Sterling was one of the first to popularize the idea of an international terrorist conspiracy to undermine the Western industrialized democracies. She wrote in 1981 that "direct control of the terrorist groups was never the Soviet intention. All are indigenous to their countries. All began as offshoots of relatively nonviolent movements that expressed particular political, economic, religious or ethnic grievances."[4] The assassination attempt against Pope John Paul II by a Turk, Mehmet Ali Agca, with alleged Bulgarian and KGB connections, stirred broader interest in the "international terrorist network. In 1983, in *The Grand Strategy of the Soviet Union*, Edward Luttwak argued that Soviet support for terrorist groups came in response to the failure of more traditional Soviet measures. It was only when it became clear that the Soviet Union was ineluctably losing the support of the trade unions and left-wing mass movements of the West that the Soviet leaders began to accept terrorists as useful allies. . . . "[5] By 1984, Ray Cline (formerly with

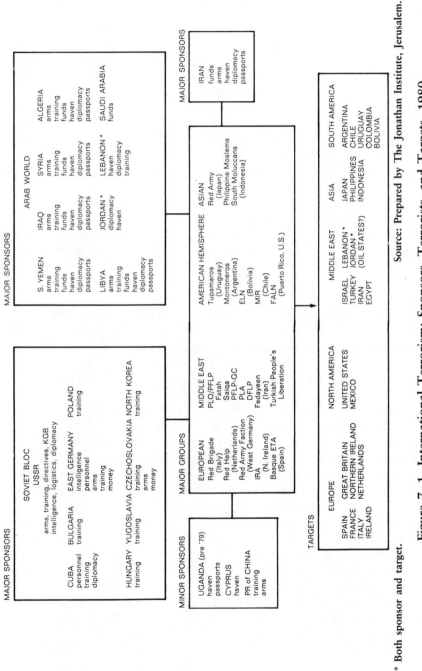

MAJOR SPONSORS

SOVIET BLOC
USSR
arms, training, directives, KGB
intelligence, logistics, diplomacy

CUBA	BULGARIA	EAST GERMANY	POLAND
personnel	training	intelligence	training
training		personnel	
diplomacy		arms	
		training	
		money	

HUNGARY YUGOSLAVIA CZECHOSLOVAKIA NORTH KOREA
training   training   training   training
                          arms
                          money

MAJOR SPONSORS

ARAB WORLD

S. YEMEN	IRAQ	SYRIA	ALGERIA
arms	arms	arms	arms
training	training	training	training
funds	funds	funds	funds
haven	haven	haven	haven
diplomacy	diplomacy	diplomacy	diplomacy
passports	passports	passports	passports

LIBYA	JORDAN *	LEBANON *	SAUDI ARABIA
arms	diplomacy	haven	funds
training	haven	diplomacy	
funds		training	
haven			
diplomacy			
passports			

MAJOR SPONSORS

IRAN
funds
arms
haven
diplomacy
passports

MINOR SPONSORS

UGANDA (pre '79)
haven
passports
CYPRUS
haven
PR of CHINA
training
arms

MAJOR GROUPS

EUROPEAN
Red Brigade
  (Italy)
Red Help
  (Netherlands)
Red Army Faction
  (West Germany)
IRA
  (N. Ireland)
Basque ETA
  (Spain)

MIDDLE EAST
PLO/PFLP
Fatah
Saiqa
PFLP-GC
PLA
DFLP
Fedayeen
  (Iran)
Turkish People's
Liberation

AMERICAN HEMISPHERE
Tupamaros
  (Uruguay)
Montoneros
  (Argentina)
ELN
  (Bolivia)
MIR
  (Chile)
FALN
  (Puerto Rico, U.S.)

ASIAN
Red Army
  (Japan)
Philippine Moslems
South Moluccans
  (Indonesia)

TARGETS

EUROPE
SPAIN
FRANCE
ITALY
IRELAND

GREAT BRITAIN
NORTHERN IRELAND
NETHERLANDS

NORTH AMERICA
UNITED STATES
MEXICO

MIDDLE EAST
ISRAEL
TURKEY
IRAN
EGYPT

LEBANON *
JORDAN *
(OIL STATES?)

ASIA
JAPAN
PHILIPPINES
INDONESIA

SOUTH AMERICA
ARGENTINA
CHILE
URUGUAY
COLOMBIA
BOLIVIA

Source: Prepared by The Jonathan Institute, Jerusalem.

Figure 7–1. International Terrorism: Sponsors, Terrorists, and Targets, 1980

* Both sponsor and target.

the CIA) and Yonah Alexander argued in *Terrorism: The Soviet Connection* that terrorism had become indispensable to the Soviets's efforts to undermine western democracies and hasten the end of capitalism.

The evidence used to support the "international terrorist network" theory is often circumstantial and open to different interpretations. Many groups that use terrorism espouse Marxist-Leninist ideology—e.g., West Germany's Red Army Faction, Italy's Red Brigades, the Irish National Liberation Army, and the Popular Front for the Liberation of Palestine (PFLP). The Soviet Union has publicly supported some of these groups in the media and at the United Nations and defended and legitimized their use of violence "in the struggle for national self-determination and against imperialism." Soviet and Eastern-bloc weapons often have been found by Western governments fighting these groups, although the international traffic in weapons undermines the persuasiveness of such evidence. The Israeli discovery of Russian maps in 1978 in Palestinian camps in Lebanon, and the 1985 capture of Nidia Diaz, commander of the Salvadoran Marxist Central American Revolutionary Workers Party, provide stronger evidence of Soviet contacts and terrorist training in Soviet and other socialist states. Nidia Diaz kept a journal that was captured with her; in it, she recorded that Salvadorans were training abroad in Bulgaria, East Germany, Vietnam, and the Soviet Union.[6] Other Western states have expelled Soviet diplomats, complaining that KGB operatives were assisting local terrorist groups. In 1978, Italy expelled twenty two Soviets for alleged ties to the Red Brigades, and in 1983 the Republic of Ireland expelled three Soviet diplomats for allegedly supplying weapons and funds to the Provisional IRA. In 1985, the Israelis announced finding evidence that thirty five Lebanese Shi'ites had been trained in small arms and explosives in the Soviet Crimea.

In addition to the Soviets or other friendly socialist states providing funds, weapons, and political support, the "international terrorist network" theory often argues that contacts or networking among different groups is instigated and facilitated by the Soviet Union or its allies. When members of the Baader-Meinhof Gang went to Lebanon and Jordan to train with the PFLP in 1970, some traveled by way of East Berlin (others went by way of Paris). The Patrice Lumumba Institute in Moscow, which offers many non-Soviets an opportunity to study on scholarship, is another means by which the Soviets allegedly put future terrorists in contact with each other. Marxist members of the Sandinista government in Nicaragua have spoken of training they received in North Korea and alongside Palestinians in Beirut in the early 1970s; and currently the presence of Cuban, East German, and Soviet advisers in Nicaragua is taken as further evidence of the Soviet conspiracy to destabilize governments in Latin America. The Palestine Liberation Organization also is identified with the Soviet Union; Chairman Arafat has made numerous visits to Moscow and has also traveled to East

Germany, Yugoslavia, Bulgaria, and Hungary, in addition to numerous meetings with Cuban officials in Beirut. Camps set up in Libya, Syria, Algeria, Iraq, Lebanon, and South Yemen to assist Palestinians training for conflict with Israel have been opened to European and Latin and North American terrorists. The British government found evidence that the assassins of Lord Mountbatten trained in a Marxist PFLP camp and the Spanish government has reported that ETA Basque terrorists have trained in Cuba and Czechoslovakia. In its campaign to arrest all RAF members in the late 1970s and early 1980s, the West German government reported finding evidence that RAF members had also trained in South Yemen and Libya, and had links to terrorist groups in Italy, France, the Netherlands, Belgium, Iran, Lebanon, and the United States.

Skeptics reject the claims of a Soviet conspiracy to fund, arm, and direct an international terrorist network. Soviet political and logistical support for the causes that some terrorist groups pursue, skeptics argue, is not sufficient evidence to support the claim of a Soviet "conspiracy." The Soviets may exploit opportunities to stir up trouble in Western or pro-Western nations, but that does not in itself constitute a conspiracy. No evidence of direct Soviet or KGB control of terrorist groups has been produced, disbelievers frequently point out. As a state favoring change in the international status quo, the Soviet Union predictably will support terrorist groups, skeptics concede, but the issues and grievances that terrorists cite are not Soviet creations. Critics of the conspiracy theory point out that the desire to believe in a communist conspiracy is very strong, even when the evidence is weak. Michael Stohl has identified the key—but dangerously circular—logic in the conspiracy theory: since the Soviet Union is an anti–status quo power, benefiting from the chaos and anarchy terrorism causes, the Soviet Union must be the source of international terrorism.[7]

In addition to the skeptics (who recognize evidence of Soviet support for terrorist groups but do not conclude that a conspiracy exists), there are several experts who conclude that the "conspiracy" theory is a Western fabrication altogether. Thomas Raynor, in *Terrorism: Past, Present, Future* (1982), argues that the Soviets shy away from groups like the RAF and Red Brigades because they are undisciplined and hurt the revolutionary cause with their brand of terrorism. Raynor recognizes Soviet and satellite aid to "wars of national liberation," but points out the lack of hard evidence of a network of terrorist groups. Alexander Cockburn contends that the terrorist network was essentially the product of "the rumor mill of a few Western propagandists talking to one another about a fantasy concocted by the C.I.A."[8] Cockburn's article, "Beat the Devil: The C.I.A.'s Master Plan," identifies discrepancies and errors in the testimony of Czech General Sejna who defected in 1968. Sejna's testimony passed through the rumor mill, and, Cockburn believes, emerged as the terror network/conspiracy theory several years later. The harshest opponent of the conspiracy is Edward S. Herman. In *The Real Terror Network*, Herman argues that the "terror network" is part of a new "red scare" designed to rally anti-Soviet sentiments in the West. The "real" terror network, according to Herman, is the one led by the United States that supports governments that rule by torture and terror. For example, the Shah of Iran used the state security force, SAVAK, to terrorize his political opponents; SAVAK was trained by the CIA. United States aid to the Nicaraguan contras, the Afghani *mujahedeen*, and the UNITA forces led by Jonas Savimbi in Angola and Namibia are also cited by the discreditors of the "international terror network" theory. Both superpowers are accused of involvement with international terrorism based on claims they support or conspire with terrorists.

United States Foreign Policy and Terrorism

What the President had in mind was nothing less than a dynamic national strategy: an action program designed to defeat the Communists without recourse to the hazard or the terror of nuclear war; one designed to defeat subversion where it had already erupted, and, even more important, to prevent its taking initial root . . . [9]

It is possible to neutralize carefully selected and planned targets, such as court judges, mesta judges, police and state Security Officials, CDS chiefs, etc.[10]

In January 1961 Nikita Khrushchev and John F. Kennedy gave speeches that reflected how U.S.-Soviet competition had begun to evolve. Khrushchev vigorously declared his intention to support wars of national liberation, and Kennedy called on the U.S. military to build a counterinsurgency program. The Soviets supported efforts to alter the international status quo, and the United States set out to train forces to preserve it. Terrorism allegedly entered the United States' foreign policy repertoire by way of the counterterror programs that became the centerpiece of the "global struggle" with communist subversion. Where the Soviet Union supports insurgencies, the United States responds by training counterinsurgency forces to meet the subversion. In this section the origins of U.S. counterinsurgency program in Vietnam will be reviewed, followed by a summary of congressional investigations led by Senator Frank Church into CIA operations alleged to have used terrorism. Recent allegations of a U.S. program to train "death squads" in Central America to terrorize subversives and their sympathizers will be reviewed, as well.

The Phoenix Program

In 1961, President Kennedy ordered five hundred military advisers to South Vietnam. The army's Special Warfare Center at Fort Bragg, North Carolina, sent four hundred of its Special Forces (Green Berets), who, with CIA personnel, set up the Civilian Irregular Defense Groups (CIDG) to train South Vietnamese villagers to protect themselves from terrorist and guerrilla attacks. Within a few years the Special Forces and CIA were working separately on counterinsurgency projects. By 1965, Special Forces were training Vietnamese in "ambushing, raiding, sabotaging and committing acts of terrorism against known VC (Viet Cong) personnel."[11] The idea of turning the enemy's use of terrorism against him had become popular. In 1965, the CIA also established its own counterterror (CT) teams. "CIA representatives recruited, organized, supplied, and directly paid CT teams, whose function was to use Viet Cong techniques of terror—assassinations, abuses, kidnappings and intimidation—against the Viet Cong leadership."[12] The CIA also established People's Action Teams (PATs) for more defensive operations, patrolling village territory at night and stopping Viet Cong forces before they reached the villagers. (The PATs have often been described as one of the most effective counterinsurgency tools devised during the Vietnam war by Americans.) The small, local programs were provided with Provincial Interrogation Centers (one in each of South Vietnam's fourty four provinces), where captured Viet Cong allegedly were tortured. By 1967, the CIA began organizing a new program that would go beyond local defense and attack the Viet Cong's political infrastructure in South Vietnam. The Phoenix Program (1968–1971) targeted the Viet Cong who were Communist party members at the provincial or national level and operated across all of South Vietnam.

The Phoenix Program coordinated South Vietnamese and American police, military, and intelligence units in a three-year assault on the Viet Cong Infrastructure (VCI). Critics of Phoenix have described it as the high point of countering terror with terror, a coordinated program of assassination and murder. The U.S. House of Representatives Foreign Operations and Government Information Subcommittee Report in 1971 gave Phoenix a mixed review, acknowledging that VC leaders and supporters were the targets, but that "many of the more than 20,000 suspected VC killed under the program known as Phoenix were actually innocent civilians who were victims of faulty intelligence."[13] William Colby, who directed the program, denied that Phoenix was intended to assassinate Viet Cong: "To call it a program of murder is nonsense. . . . They were of more value to us alive than dead, and therefore, the object was to try to get them alive."[14] Between 1968 and 1971, Phoenix accounted for 20,587 VC killed (the Government of South Vietnam reported 40,994 killed),[15] and another 28,000 captured. Stopped after 1971 when news of the program leaked to the public, Phoenix remains an early hallmark of American counterterrorism.

CIA and Political Murder

After the 1973 coup in Chile that deposed the government of Salvador Allende, the U.S. Senate began an inquiry into intelligence activities carried out by the CIA against the Chilean government. The Senate Select Committee to Study Governmental Operations with Respect to Intelligence Activities, chaired by Senator Frank Church of Idaho, investigated CIA involvement in the 1973 coup and other alleged CIA assassination plots involving foreign leaders. (The Church Committee, as it came to be known, also investigated domestic intelligence activities by the CIA, wiretapping, unauthorized storage of toxic agents, as well as the FBI and National Security Agency. See Final Report, Books I-V, Report G4-755 (April 26, 1976). The Senate concluded that the CIA had conducted a massive covert attack on Fidel Castro's government in Cuba (beginning in 1959 and peaking from 1964 to 1967), including attempts to upset the economy and assassinate Castro. CIA plots to kill Castro included cigars poisoned with botulism, diving suits contaminated with fungus, exploding sea shells, and attempts to administer LSD and other drugs to cause Castro's hair and beard to fall out. The Select Committee also found that the CIA participated in a plot to assassinate Patrice Lumumba (who was killed by Congolese enemies in 1961 before the CIA plan could be carried out), and in 1961 encouraged dissidents in the Dominican Republic who planned to assassinate President Rafael Trujillo. The Church Committee reported that a CIA official gave money to the Vietnamese generals after the 1963 coup against President Diem had begun and knew of plans in 1970 to kidnap Chile's army commander-in-chief, General Rene Schneider, who died in the aborted kidnapping.

The Church Committee also documented CIA covert action in Chile from 1962 until 1973, which culminated in the overthrow and death (possibly suicide) of Marxist President Allende. The CIA, the Select Committee recommended, should be barred from three types of covert activities:

1. All political assassinations,
2. Efforts to subvert democratic governments,
3. Support for police or other internal security forces which engage in the systematic violation of human rights.[16]

In addition to political assassinations, U.S. governmental agencies' involvement with security forces (e.g., Iran's SAVAK and the Phoenix Program in South Vietnam) that used torture and terrorism to counter political unrest and subversion came under closer scrutiny.

The United States and Counterinsurgency in Latin America: Reports of Torture, Disappearances, and Death Squads

> It is a beautiful technique. By terrorizing civilians, the army is crushing the rebellion without the need to directly confront the guerrillas. . . . Attacking the civilians is the game plan. Kill the sympathizers and you win the war.[17]

Critics of United States foreign policy in Latin America now criticize a new form of U.S. interventionism: the United States allegedly exports it counterinsurgency doctrine through schools run by the American security establishment (CIA and military forces), e.g., the School of the Americas. In what appears to be a second conspiracy theory of international terrorism, the U.S. doctrine of counterterror allegedly has become the primary military and police objective in Latin America. Rather than training police to combat crime and the military to defend against external threats, Latin American security forces have shifted their focus to subversion and insurgency. With U.S. guidance, critics argue, Latin American security forces have transformed themselves to conduct irregular, internal warfare against their own people using torture, terrorism, and mass murder to stop subversion. In his study of paramilitary and state terror in Central America, Michael McClintock (an employee of Amnesty International) presents evidence that "personnel of the CIA and U.S. regular army work closely with and perhaps control top members of the Salvadoran military responsible for formulating counter-terror policy, and directly with the intelligence agencies responsible for executing policy through torture and political murder."[18] The United States response to these allegations points out that closer U.S.-Salvadoran collaboration has helped bring right-wing paramilitary death squads under control. (The military coup was followed by a brutal phase from 1980 to 1982, with eight hundred civilian deaths a month, mostly attributed to military and right-wing death squads. The U.S. embassy in August 1987 reported that the level had decreased to twenty deaths per month.)

Similar allegations of U.S. counterinsurgency training that Latin American security forces have used against civilians have implicated previous governments in Guatemala and Argentina. Investigative journalist Jack Anderson reported in August 1981 that the United States was paying Cuban expatriates to train security forces in Guatemala, and in 1982 the *Washington Post* announced that Special Forces were training Guatemalan officers.

Following a coup in 1982, Amnesty International reported that the new regime killed twenty-six hundred peasants in its first six months in power. Guatemala elected a popular government in 1986 and death squad activity has declined, but estimates of civilian deaths since the CIA helped overthrow the government of Jacobo Arbenz in 1954 range upwards of sixty thousand.[19] The "dirty war" in Argentina (see chapter 4) that the security forces conducted from 1976 until 1983 took approximately thirty thousand lives. The mass murder and terror have been blamed in part on the "counterterror doctrine" that Argentina's military, intelligence, and police forces adopted in response to increasing terrorism from the ERP and the Montoneros. The counterinsurgency and counterterror training was provided at the Inter-American Police Academy and the School of the Americas (Panama), now closed.

Summary

Interesting parallels emerge in allegations of U.S. and Soviet sponsorship of international terrorism. The two superpowers have carried their rivalry into the turbulent politics of the Third World, where insurgency and counterinsurgency attract outside interest. For the superpowers, sponsorship or involvement in international terrorism may offer opportunities to promote their interests and influence, opportunities not available through other, more traditional channels. The temptation for the superpowers is the same one experienced by groups employing terrorism to achieve nationalist or ideological goals: important ends can be used to justify terrorist means. The documentary record remains too incomplete to conclude with any certainty that the Soviet Union or the United States sponsors international terrorism. As a potential instrument of foreign policy, however, international terrorism must be considered as part of the potential repertoire available to either the United States or the USSR in their global rivalry.

8

Terrorism and Democracy

> It must be a cardinal principle of liberal democracies in dealing with problems of civil violence and terrorism, however serious they may be, never to be tempted into using the methods of tyrants and totalitarians. Indiscriminate repression is totally incompatible with the liberal values of humanity, liberty and justice. . . . What shall it profit a liberal democracy to be delivered from the stress of factional strife only to be case under the iron heel of despotism?"[1]
> —Paul Wilkinson, *Terrorism and the Liberal State* (1986)

Authoritarian regimes, including right-wing militarist governments and left-wing (often called "totalitarian") states, are well equipped to handle terrorism because there are few limits on the governments' prerogatives. Liberal democracies, however, have struggled to find a response to terrorism that does not undermine democracy in the process of defending it. In this chapter the unique characteristics of liberal democracies that create vulnerabilities to terrorism are considered; then the responses of four particular democratic regimes to terrorism are reviewed. The Federal Republic of Germany and the United States have confronted problems of domestic terrorism, and their governments' responses to the groups using terrorism are considered respectively. Great Britain and Israel confront terrorism in territories under their control, although the problem is not wholly of a "domestic" nature; the British and Israeli response to the threat of terrorism are also reviewed. In all four cases, governments have faced difficult choices in balancing democracy and security.

The Salient Features of Liberal Democracy and Vulnerabilities to Terrorism

Out of the many studies of terrorism and democracies' responses, three characteristic features of liberal democracy and four types of vulnerability to terrorist violence consistently emerge. The liberal, democratic states share respect for

1. Government based on the consent of the governed,

2. Government by rule of law, not the arbitrary rule of men, and

3. The government's monopoly on the use of force to maintain the peace and protect the national security.[2]

These values traditionally are embodied in constitutions (written and unwritten), which also set forth individual civil rights that the government is obliged to respect. Those civil rights in effect limit the scope of actions a state can take in countering terrorism, and the same civil rights are at greater risk as the danger from terrorism increases. The temptation to suspend civil rights in an all-out fight against terrorism is strong, but to do so is to undermine or betray a central feature of a democracy. Liberal states are vulnerable to terrorism in four distinct ways as a result of their developed, democratic nature.

1. Democratic systems enjoy an "openness" that closed systems deny their citizens. "Openness" entails the right to move about (within the country or to other countries) freely and to associate with others as one chooses. Free speech and a free press are highly valued, and infringement on individuals' liberty and privacy usually are avoided. This highly valued "openness" translates into easy accessibility to vulnerable targets (human and property) when terrorists choose to strike in a democratic state. The openness that makes democratic regimes free and vital may be lost when authorities must identify and track terrorists and their supporters. Wiretapping, censorship, roadblock searches, the infiltration of suspect groups, arrest, and interrogation without warrants or public trials have been used by liberal democracies trying to combat terrorism. The valued "openness" becomes a liability during long sieges of terrorist violence, and openness is lost, at least temporarily, while the state combats terrorism.

2. The technology pioneered in the industrialized democratic states has become a weapon terrorists use to attack democratic regimes. Small and powerful light arms and explosives (many easily available from arms dealers or friendly governments, or stolen) have provided terrorist with threatening firepower. The technology of rapid transportation has provided terrorists with new mobility and new targets: subways, trains, and civil aviation. Nuclear technology has yet to yield new weapons (i.e., bombs or nuclear material to contaminate the air or water supplies of target cities or states), but nuclear power plants are considered prime, prospective targets for terrorist attack. The technology of instantaneous global communication has made radio and television coverage available to terrorists seeking to publicize causes or grievances, and helps to spread the impact of the terror their attacks are meant to create. Increasingly, democracies are learning to use technology against terrorism: metal detectors (and soon explosive sniff-

ers) help reduce the number of airline hijackings; computer networks help governments pool intelligence and track terrorist; and sophisticated surveillance technology helps government spy on terrorists.

3. A free press is highly valued in democracies as an important medium for the exchange of ideas and for monitoring state behavior. Uncensored and competitive news media, however, at times have given terrorists an open platform to terrorize the public. Great pressure subsequently builds for the government to act in order to avoid appearing impotent. The news media may become inadvertent participants in terrorism when they provide large amounts of uncritical publicity for terrorist groups. Journalists reject censorship of terrorist crises and yet are reluctant to restrain their coverage because of intense competition to "get the story." Terrorism cleverly has exploited one of the key functional components of liberal democracies: the free news media.

4. Liberal democracies operate with the consent of the governed and therefore must be sensitive to public opinion. Terrorist attacks, especially ones that receive sensational media attention, attempt to manipulate public opinion and put pressure on democratic governments to meet terrorists' demands. The public expects to be protected by its government, and terrorist attacks undermine the public's confidence in its elected officials. The media may publicize the plight of terrorists' victims or hostages, and such coverage can result in tremendous public pressure to act—whether to negotiate or retaliate may be less important than the appearance of action. Democratic governments trying to satisfy public demands to put an end to terrorism find that they must act under highly difficult conditions: public pressure is intense and crisis conditions prevail. Terrorists act, and governments must respond while also dealing with the media and public opinion. Many democratic governments have formed crisis management centers to coordinate their response and handle media requests. The scrutiny of public opinion, especially when terrorist attacks expose the vulnerabilities of democratic societies, is one factor that liberal governments cannot ignore as they formulate their response to terrorism. It is not sufficient to end a terrorist crisis; it must be ended in such a way as to merit public approval afterwards.

The four vulnerabilities of liberal democracies—(1) openness, (2) technology, (3) free media, and (4) public opinion—tend to combine to produce a double dilemma. Democratic governments that confront terrorism run the risks of overreacting and underreacting in a terrorist crisis. Democracies may overreact to terrorism and suspend civil liberties and freedom of the press in order to maximize the ability of law enforcement agencies to combat terrorism. Repressive measures such as mass arrests, brutal interrogation, and wiretapping are often effective in breaking up terrorist groups. Unfortunately, such extreme measures undermine the rule of law and civil liberties on which democratic government is based. Over the long run, the use of repressive measures to counter terrorism also risks alienating public opinion if the government appears to use methods as violent and illegitimate as those of the terrorists. A democratic government also runs the risk of underreacting—that is, appearing weak if it (1) does nothing, (2) negotiates with terrorists, or (3) concedes to their demands. U.S. presidents, for example, have been criticized for doing too little to free American hostages in Lebanon. Presidents have also been criticized for the measures they did use to obtain Americans' release, as pointed out by the U.S. Congress in the Iran-Contra Hearings, September 1987 Report. Democratic governments must try to strike the right balance between overreacting and underreacting to terrorism often under crisis conditions (lack of complete information, high risk, and limited decision-making time). Compounding their difficulties are intense media scrutiny and the need to satisfy public opinion. Terrorism creates a very difficult series of problems for democratic states. The responses of four states that confronted terrorism are considered below.

The Federal Republic of Germany's Response to the Baader-Meinhof Gang (Red Army Faction)

> The community of democrats must prove it is stronger than the perpetrators of violence.[3]
>
> Willy Brandt, speech while Hans Martin Schleyer was held hostage (September 1977)

West Germany's "baby-boom" generation came of age in the late 1960s, and as the student movement and war protests of that period lost steam the Red Army Faction became active. Jillian Becker (author of *Hitler's Children: The Story of the Baader-Meinhof Terrorist Gang*) described them as a generation that had the illusion of power to effect political change.[4] As the United States began troop withdrawals and renewed negotiations to end its role in Vietnam (1969), student radicals in West Germany adopted new goals: to trigger communist revolutions, beginning in West Germany. The Red Army Faction, which had begun its campaign by fire-bombing a department store in Frankfurt (1968), committed itself to a strategy of breaking the law repeatedly in order to "wean the masses from their habit of obedience."[5] In August 1970, after returning from PFLP training camps in Jordan, RAF members raided a NATO arsenal and set out on a series of bank robberies to finance terrorist operations. The West German government and law enforcement agencies would not undertake a serious, concerted response until 1972, when the FRG government was humiliated by the botched rescue attempt at the Munich Olympic Games.

1972 was a watershed year for terrorism in West Germany. In May, the RAF bombed police headquarters in Augsburg and Munich and two American military facilities (in Frankfurt and Heidelberg). The Axel Springer Publishing House in Hamburg also was dynamited, and police began to search in earnest for members of the terrorist group. Andreas Baader was arrested on June 1 following an anonymous tip to the police, and two weeks later the other leader of the RAF, Ulrike Meinhof, was arrested, also on a telephone tip to the police. At the end of the summer, the Olympic Games began in Munich with the local Bavarian police in charge of security. (Under West Germany's postwar constitution, the police forces were decentralized and the state police agency, the *Bundeskriminalamt* (BKA) was barred from supervising Olympic security efforts.) The local police were not well prepared to handle the terrorist crisis that began when the Palestinian group, Black September, took Israeli athletes hostage. Poor intelligence and inadequate training resulted in a gun battle at night between the terrorists and police in which all the hostage Israeli athletes died. The tragic fiasco forced the West German government to recognize that it was not prepared to deal with terrorism. When the RAF issued a statement praising Black September's attack in a communiqué titled "Die Aktion des schwarzen September in München" later that month, the Bonn government was reminded that it faced both domestic and international threats of terrorism. The government set in motion a long series of legislative and other policy initiatives to deal with terrorism, including

1. Creation of the elite, antiterrorist unit, GSG9;
2. Tighter airport security measures;
3. Telephone hotlines for informers to leave anonymous tips on terrorists;
4. Harsher prison terms for specific terrorist offenses;
5. Emergency antiterrorist laws that permit detention without trial;
6. News media censorship;
7. Computing intelligence on terrorists and strengthening the BKA; and
8. A concerted police effort to break up the RAF via roadblocks, wiretaps, infiltration, and other controversial methods.

Many of the measures initiated in Bonn were received with unanimous public approval. Better security measures were implemented at West German airports and hotlines for informants were well received. The *Grenzschutzgruppe 9* (Border Protection Group 9) was created to provide the FRG with an elite force trained and equipped to resolve terrorist crises. The first GSG9 leader, Ulrich Wegener, who trained with the Israelis' General Intelligence and Reconnaissance Unit 269, set the elite unit up in six groups of thirty volunteers each; GSG9 teams trained as marksmen, technical experts, and commandos. The GSG9 enjoyed its first major success in 1977 when it stormed a Lufthansa airliner that had been hijacked to Mogadishu, Somalia, and safely freed all hostages aboard. West Germany's reputation, tarnished by previous negotiations with terrorists and the Munich Olympics debacle, was instantly restored by the GSG9 rescue mission. (British Special Air Service, SAS, supplied the blinding stun grenades that the West Germans used.) The Bonn government also began writing legislation in 1976 to increase fines and prison terms (up to thirty-two years) for publishing terrorist manuals (e.g., "how-to" instructional guides for building bombs) or engaging in terrorist activities.

In 1977, West Germany took a series of controversial steps in its campaign against terrorism. During the Mogadishu hijacking and the kidnapping of Hans Martin Schleyer, the Federal Republic obtained the cooperation of nearly the entire news industry in blacking out all coverage of those crises in progress. The 1987 capture of Lebanese terrorists in West Germany and kidnapping of FRG nationals in Lebanon received similar black-out treatment. This censorship was and is now hotly debated among journalistic circles, although it is generally accepted by the public at large.

In addition to the censorship that the West German media helped implement, the Bonn government also began a counteroffensive to arrest RAF members within the country and abroad. Using wiretaps, opening mail, setting up random roadblocks to check identity papers, and keeping suspects under surveillance, the West German police coordinated their efforts to put the RAF out of action. In Bulgaria, government agents located several terrorists who were brought back to West Germany against their will and without benefit of formal extradition hearings. Once in custody, antiterrorist legislation allowed German authorities to hold suspects awaiting trial for up to five years, because "terrorist conspiracy" had been legally designated a "major crime" and suspected terrorists were considered a threat to society. (The antiterrorist laws have not been repealed.)

Two of the most hotly contested pieces of legislation the government passed after the arrest of dozens of RAF members authorized West German authorities to (1) read client-attorney correspondence and (2) to limit the number of attorneys defending RAF suspects. Authorities in Stuttgart were accused of electronically eavesdropping on privileged client-attorney conversations, and Arab students and "guest workers" have complained of surveillance and infiltration of their various organizations.

In addition to passing legislation empowering much more aggressive pursuit and prosecution of terrorists, the West German government also modified its bureaucracy to better combat terrorism. Prospective employees of the FRG Civil Service (which accounts for 13 percent of West German employment)[6] have been required since 1972 to report whether they are or have been affiliated with any extremist organization. Known as the Radicals Ordinance (*Radikalenerlass*), any person suspected of disloyalty can be barred from government employment. The Bonn government has continued to strengthen the central police force, augmenting the BKA staff from fifteen hundred at the time of the Munich Olympic Games to over twenty-five hundred,[7] as well as improving coordination between the ten Lander police forces, West Berlin's police, and the Federal Criminal Investigation Office. Each police force has a commando or SWAT unit, and the forces have access to a central computer at the Interior Ministry that compiles all available data on terrorism and radical groups. Finally, to safely prosecute the dozens of RAF members arrested, West Germany built a special prison and courtroom in Stammheim, outside Stuttgart. Because of the RAF history of escapes and attacks on state prosecutors, a high-security facility was built at a cost of over DM 12 million.[8]

The measures taken by the FRG to combat RAF terrorism, and to keep some of its alien population under surveillance, have been well received by the general public. Some have even called for restoration of the death penalty for terrorist crimes. The hottest debate over the government's response to terrorism has occurred in European, American, and West German academic, legal, and journalistic circles. At the time of the 1977 Mogadishu rescue by GSG9 a wave of anti-German hostility swept across Europe, with articles describing a new "springtime for Hitler" and "lynch mob"[9] rules. Melvin Lasky, writing in the *New York Times*, drew comparisons between the policies of Willy Brandt and the Nazis[10] as early as 1975, and a vocal if relatively small number of Germans have condemned the violation of civil liberties over the course of the campaign against the RAF. West German attorneys have complained bitterly of the violation of attorney-client privileged communcation, and journalists note the ready cooperation between the news industry and government to black out coverage of terrorism. On the other hand, the antiterrorist emergency laws and other state policies have been very well received by the German public. No election has raised the issue of overreacting to terrorism and thereby imperiling democracy; to the contrary, the German public has supported government efforts to end terrorism and restore "law and order." The tension between national security and civil liberties appears to favor security concerns at this point in the West German response to terrorism.

United States' Response to Terrorism: The Black Panthers, the Symbionese Liberation Army, and the Weather Underground

Like West Germany in the late 1960s, the United States also saw its "baby-boom" generation join student movements and war protests on the nation's

campuses. The civil rights movement had activated the political conscious-
ness of America's minorities, and radical black groups added their voice to
the protests and demonstrations. After the assassination of Dr. Martin
Luther King in 1968, followed by the violence at the Democratic National
Convention in Chicago (where war protesters were forcibly excluded from
participating), the protests became more violent and some groups turned to
terrorism. As the Church Committee reported in its 1976 analysis, the
dissidence and terrorism would provoke "an unprecedented, coordinated,
illegal effort to use the weapons of the U.S. espionage establishment against
American citizens."[11] That effort followed presidential orders to the CIA to
investigate whether dissident groups were influenced or directed by foreign
powers (Operation Chaos). The FBI, meanwhile, continued its efforts to
disrupt or neutralize American "subversives" in a program that began in
1946 called COINTELPRO. (Looking for communists had replaced the war
against organized crime as the FBI's primary task; the "New Left" and
dissident groups were the foci of FBI efforts to locate communists since the
earliest days of the Cold War.) By 1970, the SDS, the Weather Underground, and black militant groups, especially the Black Panthers, became
the targets of some of the most drastic counterterrorism measures ever
taken inside the United States during peacetime. The Church Committee
reported finding "a pattern of reckless disregard of activities that threatened our Constitutional system."[12] In retrospect, several basic democratic
values were at risk as the intelligence and security community responded to
the terrorism problem in the late 1960s and early 1970s, especially the
fourth amendment to the Constitution: "the right of the people to be secure
in their persons, houses and papers and effects against unreasonable
searches and seizures shall not be violated, and no warrant shall issue, but
upon probable cause, supported by oath or affirmation, and particularly
describing the place to be searched and the persons or things to be seized."

**Student Protest and Antiwar Groups: The Students for a Democratic Soci-
ety (SDS) and the Weather Underground.** Like the Baader-Meinhof Gang,
the Weathermen (called the Weatherpeople or the Weather Underground
after 1970 out of respect for its feminist membership) emerged from a
student protest movement, part of which evolved into a violent, revolutionary organization. The roots of the Weather Underground lay in the liberal
Students for a Democratic Society, established in 1960. Throughout the
early 1960s SDS had become increasingly more radical following the assassination of John F. Kennedy and growing American involvement in the
Vietnam war. Some Marxists and Maoists joined SDS, but as the peace
demonstrations and draft protests escalated into more violent attacks on
induction centers and confrontations with police, the violent revolutionaries

broke with SDS to form the Weather Underground. In 1969, a group led by Bernadine Dohrn and Mark Rudd left SDS, and in the paper "You Don't Need a Weatherman to Know Which Way the Wind Blows," they declared their intentions: to follow a course of "immediate and drastic militancy" and to use terror in the struggle against the American "establishment." In their National Action plan, terrorism held a central role in what was to be an explosive campaign to trigger revolution by "the oppressed masses." For four days in October 1969 in the "Days of Rage," the Weather Underground held rallies and rampaged through Chicago. Denounced by SDS, the Weather Underground proceeded to conduct a terror campaign of bombings against police stations, government, and military facilities. In its 1974 publication *Prairie Fire*, the Weather Underground described its intentions: "Our final goal is the destruction of imperialism, the seizure of power and the creation of socialism." The United States government took them seriously, and the FBI investigated every member of SDS and the Weather Underground. As in the Federal Republic of Germany, files were kept so that "the information could be used if they ever applied for a government job."[13] Until most of its members were arrested or went underground in 1975, the Weather Underground used bombs to protest the Vietnam War and later simply to attack "the system." Their bombings, usually accompanied by a telephoned warning to evacuate, included attacks on

New York City and Detroit police stations (1970),

U S. Army Mathematical Research Center, University of Wisconsin (Madison) (1970),

Police statue in Haymarket Square, Chicago (1970),

Courthouses in California and Long Island (1970),

The Senate men's restroom, U.S. Capitol (1971)

The Pentagon (1972),

ITT corporate offices (1973), and

U.S. Department of State (1975).

The Weather Underground, with over fifty groups[14] operating across the country, took credit for twenty-five bombings in five years in *Osawatomie*, a magazine it published in 1975. It supported the efforts of the militant Black Panther Party and announced its approval of the 1974 kidnapping of heiress Patricia Hearst by the Symbionese Liberation Army. The Weather Underground also was responsible for a raid on the National Guard Armory in Boston to steal weapons in 1970 and later that year helped LSD guru and former Harvard psychologist Timothy Leary escape from prison in San Luis Obispo, California. The Weather Underground received headline coverage from the media and was targeted by the FBI for wiretapping and infiltration. By the late 1970s, with the Vietnam war concluded and the revolutionary fires doused on American campuses, Weather Underground members were disbanded, in jail, or underground. The record of the response their terrorist acts provoked would be uncovered by the Church Committee investigations (see below) shortly thereafter.

The Black Panthers and Terrorism

> The Black Panther Party has publicly advertised its goals of organizing revolution, insurrection, assassination and other terrorist—type activities.[15]

The Black Panthers were organized in Oakland, California, by Huey Newton and Bobby Seale in 1966. The peaceful phase of the black civil rights movement, with its voter registration drives and nonviolent demonstrations, was ending, and growing emphasis was placed on black power and black militancy. The Student Non-Violent Coordinating Committee (SNCC), which began as a civil rights group in North Carolina, became more militant—but not militant enough as members Stokeley Carmichael and H. Rap Brown shifted their support to the paramilitary Black Panthers' separatist, antiwhite ideology.

In 1966, Huey Newton and Bobby Seale announced their goals: "We want land, bread, housing, education, clothing, justice and peace."[16] The Black Panthers, like Ireland's Provisional IRA, also announced they would "protect" the local population against police brutality. Joined by Eldridge Cleaver, author of *Soul on Ice*, the Black Panthers became "the greatest threat to the internal security of the country,"[17] according to the FBI. In 1967, armed Black Panthers invaded the California State Legislature, and gun battles with police took place on the streets of Oakland. Following the assassination of Dr. Martin Luther King in 1968, the shift to revolutionary ideology and violence took on added energy. Black Panthers began traveling abroad (Cuba, Soviet Union, North Korea, Algeria) and voicing an increasingly hostile revolutionary rhetoric. In 1969, police arrested twenty Black Panthers on charges of conspiracy to bomb bridges, buildings, and tunnels in New York. The SDS lauded the Black Panthers as "the vanguard of black liberation," while the FBI targeted them for harassment, wiretapping, and infiltration. FBI and police forces, working together, arrested Black Panthers across the country, and membership dropped from twelve hundred in 1969 to seven hundred in 1972.[18] Eldridge Cleaver fled to Algeria, Bobby Seale renounced violence, while a new, even more violent black group appeared to fill the void: the Black Liberal Army (BLA).

The BLA said it was dedicated to terrorizing police who terrorized the black community. With slogans like, "Destiny lies in the bloody death of racist pigs,"[19] BLA members supported themselves by robberies and drug dealing. The BLA murdered its first police victim in 1971 and was active through 1973. Only a few hundred strong, the BLA was put out of action by police and FBI agents after it had claimed—by its own count—eight victims in two years. (The FBI has not published the number of police deaths it ascribed to the BLA.) Like the student protest and antiwar movements, militant black groups began to lose impetus as the Vietnam war wound down, and police and FBI efforts against militant groups increased. As the student protest, antiwar, and black liberation terrorism subsided and law enforcement agencies (and the general public) thought domestic terrorism was ending, one last spasm of terrorism occurred with the bizarre Symbionese Liberation Army's year of terror.

The Symbionese Liberation Army: Terrorism of the Seven-Headed Cobra

Death to the fascist insect that preys upon the life of the people[20]

The Symbionese Liberation Army grew out of the interaction between black inmates at the Vacaville State Prison (near San Francisco) and white, middle-class Berkeley students who traveled to the prison to participate in therapeutic "rap sessions." Donald DeFreeze escaped from prison and took refuge with some of the students, forming the Symbionese Liberation Army of Revolutionary War and Symbionese Program in August 1973. *Symbionese* referred to the symbiosis or harmonious coexistence of races and classes that would follow the revolution of the oppressed that the SLA planned to provoke and then to lead. The group made a seven-headed cobra its trademark, representing the union of black, brown, red, yellow, and white races with both young and old members. (At other times members said the seven heads stood for self-determination, cooperative production, creativity, unity, faith, purpose, and collective responsibility.)[21] One of the SLA members, Joseph Remiro, was a Vietnam veteran who trained the ten-member organization in marksmanship. They prepared a hit list of officials and businessmen marked for kidnapping and execution, and began their campaign of terror by murdering Oakland school superintendent, Marcus Foster, in November 1973. The bullets that killed him were filled with cyanide, and the SLA took credit for the murder in a letter sent to a local radio station. Despite its sometimes confused ideology, the SLA had a keen instinct for obtaining publicity.

After announcing their war on the "fascist, capitalist class" and getting little in the way of public support or new members, DeFreeze (now calling himself Field Marshall Cinque) and his followers planned a sensational kidnapping to bring them publicity and popularity. On February 4, 1974, the SLA kidnapped Patricia Hearst, daughter of newspaper publisher, Randolph Hearst, and demanded a multimillion dollar food giveaway in exchange for her release. This was intended to make the SLA popular heroes and to generate more media attention. Through communiqués to the same radio station (KPFA), the SLA made additional demands, released tapes of Patty Hearst's pleas to her parents, and eventually announced her "conversion" to the SLA cause. Patty Hearst adopted the name Tania, after Ché Guevara's lover and companion, and soon brought the SLA bountiful publicity. Participating in a bank robbery in April 1974, Patty Hearst became a cult figure while over a hundred FBI agents searched for her. The SLA was finally located in May in Los Angeles, where their safehouse was surrounded by police who had received a tip on their whereabouts. A gunbattle ensued with over six thousand shots fired,[22] and the house burned to the ground, but Patty Hearst and two other SLA members were not among the dead. "Tania" went underground and was not captured until September 1975. She was tried and convicted of armed robbery, bringing to a close one of the more curious chapters in American terrorism.

United States Response to Domestic Terrorism

> The Committee has found excesses committed by intelligence agencies—lawless and improper behavior, intervention in the democratic process, overbroad intelligence targeting and collection, and the use of covert techniques to discredit and "neutralize" persons and groups defined as enemies by the agencies.[23]

The United States Senate Select Committee to Study Governmental Operations with Regard to Intelligence, chaired by Senator Frank Church, initially began its investigation of the intelligence community by looking into the CIA's role in the 1973 fall of Salvador Allende's Chilean government. The investigation expanded to include domestic intelligence activities, from CIA involvement in the Watergate scandal to the FBI's programs to disrupt and discredit "subversive" groups. The Church Committee reported finding serious breaches of law and violations of democratic values, what Frank Church called "malignant plots [that] grew out of the obsessions of the Cold War."[24] American groups that protested the Vietnam war and, later, groups that employed terrorism to provoke revolutions were the targets of concerted programs to identify and disrupt so-called subversive activity. Specifically, the FBI's COINTELPRO (Counterintelligence Program) and the CIA's Operation Chaos targeted subversive groups for surveillance and dirty tricks, while the White House planned to coordinate the entire intelligence community's covert operations against dissidents. (The Huston Plan, as it was known, was never implemented.)

COINTELPRO. When the Church Committee reviewed the history of the FBI's domestic intelligence activities, it found that the FBI had been given broad and vague instructions (in presidential directives as early as 1936) to collect data on "subversive activities." The Church Committee Report also noted that the FBI, which originally concentrated on foreign threats and groups thought to be under Communist influence, had expanded the scope of Bureau surveillance to include civil rights and antiwar groups. The FBI developed over five hundred thousand domestic intelligence files[25] on American citizens and groups and opened sixty-five thousand files[26] in 1972 alone. The FBI also kept a list of twenty-six thousand individuals to be rounded up in case of a "national emergency." In addition to the excesses in collecting intelligence, the Church Committee reported that the FBI conducted illegal covert actions against American citizens and used illegal surveillance techniques. Over two hundred "black bag" jobs[28] were conducted against left-wing or liberal organizations to gather documents or plant listening devices. Some individuals, including Dr. Martin Luther King, were subjected to every intelligence-gathering technique the FBI had in order to gather information that could be used to discredit them. Dirty tricks, including falsely labeling individuals as FBI informants or sending letters to discredit their character, were used and mail was opened and photographed. The Church Committee found that although attorneys general authorized most wiretappings and surveillance, they did not supervise the uses to which such intelligence was put.

OPERATION CHAOS. The Central Intelligence Agency, responding to President Johnson's request, set up a Special Operations Group in 1967 to collect, coordinate, and analyze intelligence regarding foreign influence on domestic dissident groups. The group was called Operation Chaos, and over six years' time the CIA assembled thirteen thousand files and related materials that included the names of three hundred thousand people and organizations.[29] Like the FRG security forces, the CIA put all this data into computerized files. Those files were used to generate three thousand memoranda to the FBI,[30] although the CIA was not found to have used surveillance or wiretappings against American citizens in Operation Chaos. Operation Chaos, nonetheless, unlawfully exceeded the CIA's authority, which does not include internal security tasks. The Church Committee report expressed concern that the CIA had become a repository of information on the domestic activities of Americans. Apart from Operation Chaos, the CIA had a file of over one million names[31] in an index built from mail it had opened and photographed. Operation Chaos ended in 1974, shortly before the Church Committee investigations began.

THE HUSTON PLAN. In 1970, the American political scene was alive with protests, demonstrations, and violence. The Weather Underground, Black

Panthers, and antiwar protests combined to create an "internal security threat" in the eyes of Thomas Huston, an attorney on the White House staff and assistant to presidential aide Robert Haldeman. Huston participated in the Ad Hoc Interagency Committee on Intelligence, which included FBI Director J. Edgar Hoover (chair), Director of Central Intelligence Richard Helms, Defense Intelligence Agency head Donald Bennett, and National Security Agency head Admiral Noel Gaylor. Huston prepared a draft plan to assess the "current internal security threat" posed by antiwar groups, terrorist groups, black militant groups, and other revolutionary groups in the United States. Second, he proposed a plan to better coordinate the intelligence community's efforts to monitor and disrupt dissident activities. President Nixon approved the plan in June 1970 but later withdrew his approval on the advice of Attorney General John Mitchell and FBI Director J. Edgar Hoover.

The Church Committee discussed the Huston Plan in its report to illustrate the potential danger of a centralized, domestic security apparatus that could monitor and interfere with the political activities of American citizens. The Church Committee report, however, viewed the Huston Plan in the context of COINTELRPO and Operation Chaos, all of which were considered part of an ongoing effort by the intelligence community to expand domestic surveillance. In their urgent desire to counter communism at home, the various intelligence agencies did not draw fine distinctions between dissident groups and terrorist organizations. The NAACP and the Women's Liberation Movement, as well as the Weather Underground and Black Panthers, were monitored. Threats to civil liberties (i.e., privacy, free speech, and freedom of association) were threatened by the response of the intelligence community to dissidence and domestic terrorism. Given the intense publicity attending terrorism, public concern about security and intelligence agencies' eagerness to expand their domestic activities, American civil liberties were at serious risk as the state responded to terrorism in the late 1960s and early 1970s.

The United Kingdom's Response to Terrorism in Northern Ireland

It must be recognized that while the Special Powers Act created the opportunity for violations of civil liberties, that opportunity was miniscule when juxtaposed with the potential deprivation of civil liberties resulting from the imposition of violence and death.[32]

When times are normal and fear is not stalking the land, English law sturdily protects the freedom of individuals and respects human personality. But when times are abnormally alive with fear and prejudice, the

common law is at a disadvantage. It cannot resist the will, however frightened and prejudiced it may be, of Parliament. . .[33]

In the late 1960s Northern Ireland also saw a civil rights movement
deteriorate into terrorism. The Northern Ireland Civil Rights Association
(NICRA) organized marches and demonstrations in 1968 and 1969 modeled after the black civil rights movement in the United States. Unfortunately, these efforts to work peacefully within the system to improve the lot
of Catholics in Northern Ireland triggered a violent reaction from militant
Protestants. In August 1968, the NICRA was prohibited from staging public marches. When it disregarded the order and marched anyway, Royal
Ulster Constables batoned the marchers. In January 1969, on a civil rights
walk from Belfast to Londonderry the procession was ambushed by Protestant vigilantes; the RUC watched but did not intervene. The attack was
followed by several developments that contributed to the resurgence of
terrorism. (1) Rioting, intercommunal violence between Protestants and
Catholics, and police behavior in the rioting led to the perception that the
police (RUC) were neither protecting Catholics nor arresting Protestants in
the chaos. (2) The Provisionals split from the official IRA, promising to
protect Catholics from the rioting. (3) Protestant paramilitary groups increased and became more radical and violent; the Reverend Ian Paisley's
Ulster Protestant Volunteers were eclipsed by the Ulster Defense Association, the Ulster Freedom Fighters and the Ulster Volunteer Force. (4) As the
violence continued unabated, Britain decided to send troops to Northern
Ireland (1969) to try to interrupt the violence. The British troops would
become targets of and participants in the terrorism afflicting Ulster, which
continued to escalate after the troops arrived.

Deaths by Political Violence in Northern Ireland[34]

1969	13
1970	25
1971	173
1972	467
1973	250
1974	216
1975	247
1976	295
1977	112
1978	81
1979	113
1980	76
1981	101
1982	97
1983	77
1984	64

The British Response. After its 1969 decision to send troops to Northern Ireland, in 1971 Parliament was asked by Brian Faulker, Prime Minister of Northern Ireland, to resume the internment (imprisonment without public trial) of suspected terrorists. After acceding to this request, Parliament undertook a series of legislative reforms to provide the British troops in Northern Ireland with newer legal tools to combat terrorism. The new laws replaced older legislation, in particular, the Civil-Authorities (Special Powers) Act of 1922 whereby Catholics had been interned since the partition of the island. The Special Powers Act had authorized the Minister of Home Affairs or any RUC officer to "take all such steps and issue all such orders as may be necessary for preserving the peace and maintaining order."[35] The Special Powers included the right to search any person or place without a warrant; to arrest any person or seize any property without a warrant; to disperse public assemblies; to censor any printed material; and to detain any person up to forty eight hours for questions, as long as such actions were meant to prevent behavior "prejudicial to the peace." After introducing British troops, Parliament realized that such powers, and more, should be made available to the British army in Northern Ireland to combat terrorism. Parliament reached this conclusion after numerous complaints of the "illegal" arrests made by British troops in the first waves of internment. (In the first six months—August 1971 to January 1972—2,357 people were arrested, 159 were detained up to four days, and 598 were interned.)[36] There followed a series of legislative actions to give the army legal powers that went beyond those granted local authorities in the Special Powers Act of 1922. The legislation included (1) the Northern Ireland (Emergency Provisions) Act of 1973, 1975, and 1978 and (2) the Prevention of Terrorism (Temporary Provisions) Act of 1974 and 1976. The measures were hotly debated in Parliament, where concern was expressed over their "corrosive" effect on the rule of law, especially due process and habeas corpus, in Northern Ireland.

While Parliament was debating the first phase of the new legislation (the Detention of Terrorists Order), the *London Sunday Times* sent its investigative "Insight" team to observe the first stages of internment (from November 1971 to January 1972). In this early phase of the army's involvement, the *Times* concluded that the misuse of internment (for harassment, intelligence-gathering, and abuse of internees) was driving middle-class Catholics "into the arms" of the Provisional IRA. The *Times* asked if Parliament were not "seeking a military solution to the crisis at a moral price that was too high to bear?"[37] The *Times* did not provoke an intense public debate over internment or other measures Parliament was considering, nor did the government's decision to derogate from its commitments under the European Convention on Human Rights. (Internment violated the Convention, and Britain had to declare an emergency to take legal exception from its provisions.) The powers that Parliament gave to the police and the British army to counter terrorism in Ulster included the following (from the Northern Ireland Emergency Provisions Act 1973, Chapter 53):

Trials for certain "scheduled" offenses can be conducted without a jury (Part I, No. 2).

A person charged with a "scheduled" offense (including murder, manslaughter, arson, rioting, assault, possession of explosives or firearms, theft, or "aiding, abetting or inciting" commitment of such an offense) can be denied bail. (Part I, No. 3).

Written statements can be used as evidence by the state without supporting oral testimony (Part I, No. 5).

Confessions can be used as evidence; if the accused asserts that torture was used to induce the confession, the accused must prove that torture took place (Part I, No. 6).

Any constable may arrest without warrant any person whom he suspects of being a terrorist (Part II, No. 10:1).

For the purpose of arresting a person under this section, a constable may enter and search any premises or other place where that person is or where the constable suspects him of being (Part II, No. 10:2).

A constable may seize anything that he suspects is being, has been, or is intended to be used in the commission of a scheduled offense or an offense under the act that is not a scheduled offense (Part II, No. 11:3).

A member of Her Majesty's forces on duty may arrest without warrant, and detain for not more than four hours, a person whom he suspects of committing, have committed, or being about to commit any offense (Part II, No. 12:1).

A member of Her Majesty's forces may enter and search any premises for a person suspected of terrorism (Part II, No. 12:3) or any dwelling for the purpose of ascertaining whether there are any munitions stored unlawfully at that place (Part II, No. 13:1).

Any member of Her Majesty's forces on duty or any constable may stop and question any person about his identity and movements and what he knows concerning any recent explosion or other incident endangering life (Part II, No. 16:1).

Any person who fails to stop when required to do so under this section, or who refuses or fails to answer to the best of his knowledge and ability, shall be liable to six months' imprisonment and a fine of £400 (Part II, No. 16:2).

No person shall without permission collect, record, publish, or seek any information regarding the police or Her Majesty's forces that is likely to be useful to terrorists (Part III, No. 20).

In this act, except so far as the context otherwise requires, *constable* includes any member of the Royal Naval, Military or Air Forces (Part IV, No. 28).

Proscribed Organizations (Schedule 2) include the Irish Republican Army, Sinn Fein, and the Ulster Volunteer Force.

While Parliament was drafting the Emergency Provisions, internment continued in Northern Ireland and reports of abuse and torture during internment increased. (Internment would continue through 1975.) The Republic of Ireland, the NICRA, Amnesty International, the Association for Legal Justice, and the London-based National Council for Civil Liberties called for inquiries into human rights violations in Northern Ireland between 1971 and 1973. Meanwhile, the violence began to spread from Ulster to England. In 1974, over fifteen thousand British troops were in Northern Ireland when a series of bombings occurred in England. In June 1974, a twenty-pound bomb exploded in Westminster, and in July the Tower of London was bombed. That autumn, explosions in two bars in Birmingham killed twenty-one people and injured another 180; public concern soon brought demands for Parliament to take action against terrorism. The government's response was embodied in the Prevention of Terrorism Act of 1974 and 1976, in which Parliament extended the powers of search and arrest to British Constables throughout the United Kingdom. The police were authorized to detain terrorist suspects for forty-eight hours. The Secretary of State was given the power to extend detention an additional five days. The authorities also were given the power to exclude any suspected terrorist from entry into the country, and the IRA was outlawed in Britain. There was heated public debate and discussion in Parliament over restoring the dealth penalty for terrorists, but Parliament did not take that last step.

The Prevention of Terrorism Bill was enacted in November 1974 and was criticized both for doing "too little" and for going too far. In *Political Crime in Europe*, Barton Graham observed that

> what is surprising—if not shocking—to the foreign observer in the light of English history in the preceding century, is the alacrity with which the English surrendered practically the totality of their cherished liberties to the discretion of government officials during an emergency. Formerly, the temporary suspension of the regular procedures of law had been deemed all right for the Irish perhaps, but never for the English. . . .[38]

Both terrorism and antiterrorist policies in Northern Ireland had spilled over to England. From the introduction of British troops (1969), to resumption of internment (1971), to the imposition of direct rule (1972), Britain has grown more and more deeply involved. With the extension of antiterrorist legislation to England (1974), the impact on its legal system became visible. Following several internal and external reports, the human impact, in terms of human rights abuses, also became clear.

Human Rights and British Antiterror Measures in Northern Ireland. "No one shall be subjected degrading treatment or punishment" was the Article 3 declaration of the European Convention on Human Rights. The United Kingdom is a party to the Universal Declaration of Human Rights and has signed both the United Nations Covenant on Civil and Political Rights and the European Convention for the Protection of Human Rights and Fundamental Freedoms. The government of the Republic of Ireland filed the first complaint of British abuses of human rights with the European Commission in 1971, alleging Britain had violated the European Convention by failing "to secure for all persons within its jurisdiction the rights and freedoms" guaranteed by that convention. Ireland accused Britain of mistreating and torturing internees and submitted written evidence regarding 228 cases. The European Commission investigated a sample from the 228 cases and concluded that there had been a practice of inhuman and degrading treatment during the interrogation of prisoners[39] The National Council for Civil Liberties, the Northern Ireland Civil Rights Association, and the Association for Legal Justice filed a sixty-page complaint with U.N. Secretary General Kurt Waldheim in July 1973, demanding an investigation of British policies in Northern Ireland, while Amnesty International had been documenting complaints from Northern Ireland of human rights violations since 1971 (i.e., the onset of internment). That same year, Amnesty International submitted a Memorandum to the Parker Committee, which had been appointed by the British Prime Minister "to consider whether, and if so in what respects, the procedures currently authorized for the interrogation of persons suspected of terrorism and for their custody while subject to interrogation required amendment." Amnesty International cited reports of threats; beatings; deprivation of food and sleep; exposure to excessive noise, darkness, and light; and other interrogation methods allegedly used in Northern Ireland that violated internees' human rights.

In 1977, after continued reports of mistreatment and torture during internment, Amnesty International conducted a formal inquiry in Northern Ireland. The mission interviewed fifty-two persons who alleged mistreatment or torture and looked at medical records and corroborative evidence of twenty-six other cases. The alleged human rights abuses included psychologically exhausting, prolonged interrogation sessions; physically exhausting procedures (e.g., forcing a prisoner to run in place for lengthy periods or stand four to five hours continuously); threats of rape, beating, death, and threats against family members; beatings to the body and extremities; direct beatings to the head; humiliation by being forced to undress before interrogators; and other forms of torture, including hooding, choking, and being burned with a cigarette. The Amnesty International Mission, in its 1978 report, concluded that there was a general consistency between the allegations and the medical evidence, supporting the testimony of mistreatment and torture. The Amnesty Internation report indicated that the pattern of abuse in Northern Ireland was analogous to accounts given by torture victims in other AI investigations.

In response to the AI report and continuing publicity of allegations of torture in Northern Ireland, the British government commissioned the Bennett Report on interrogation procedures (completed and presented in March 1979). The report concluded that there was evidence of mistreatment (bruising, hyperextended joints, ruptured eardrums, and excessive anxiety states) among internees.[40] Female prisoners were often interviewed only by male officers, the report noted, and interrogators had no code of conduct. Specifically, the report recommended that the following practices should be prohibited:

1. Ordering prisoners to strip,
2. Requiring prisoners to adopt any unnatural or humiliating posture,
3. Requiring a prisoner to carry out unnecessarily physically exhausting actions or postures,
4. Using threats of physical force,
5. Using threats of sexual assault.[41]

The report also recommended that interrogators always wear identification badges and that the training and supervision of interrogators ought to be improved. The possibility of videotaping all interrogations was mentioned, in addition to the use of "spyholes" to improve the monitoring process. Without admitting any specific acts of torture or mistreatment, the Bennett Report offered a list of sixty-four principal conclusions and recommendations that speak to most of the allegations of torture since 1971.

For Britain, the encounter with terrorism in Northern Ireland has proven costly in terms of human lives and democratic values. Remarkably, the documentary record that provided the evidence for Amnesty International and the European Commission to condemn human rights abuses in Northern Ireland has been acknowledged by Parliament. Allegations of mistreatment and abuse have declined, although violence marks the anniversary of internment each August. In 1987, riots in Belfast, bombs in

Derry (Londonderry), homemade grenades, and bonfires indicated that deeply divided Northern Ireland has not yet recovered from internment, and the British army remains, too, daily proof of the unsolved problem of terrorism.

Israel's Response to Terrorism in the Occupied Territories

> As President Lincoln did during the American Civil War, as the United States did during World War II, and as the British found it necessary to do in Northern Ireland, the Israelis have found that in the interests of national security certain civil liberties have to be suspended.[42]

> Armed struggle is the only way to liberate Palestine. *Palestinian National Charter*, art. 9 (1968)

Like the Federal Republic of Germany, the United States, and the United Kingdom, the government of Israel confronted a terrorism problem in the late 1960s. The problem manifested itself, as it had in Europe and the United States, primarily in bombings, ambushes, and assassinations. (At the height of the terrorism, Israel witnessed sixty bombings each month in 1970 and 1971 in the Occupied Territories.)[44] Unlike the West German, American, and British experiences, however, Israel's problem with Palestinian terrorism is part of a larger continuing threat posed by surrounding Arab states that also desire the destruction of the Israeli state. Israel's is the most serious terrorist threat to national security confronting a liberal democracy today. Israel's response to terrorism has been to create a massive, integrated system of countermeasures backed up by a tough, clear philosophy about terrorism. Israel has been dealing with this problem on a daily basis since its inception, and today Israel is looked on by many as *the* model democratic states should copy when they decide to "get tough" with terrorists.

Israel: Born Out of Terrorism and War. In 1917, Great Britain announced its support for the establishment in Palestine of a "national home" for the Jewish people. The civil and religious rights of existing non-Jewish communities in Palestine were not to be prejudiced in any way. In 1922, Britain received a mandate from the League of Nations to replace Turkish control of the areas the British called Transjordan and Palestine. To assuage resident Palestinian fears, Britain announced its opposition to a Jewish state in the area, emphasizing its support only for a Jewish homeland. Nonetheless, by this time Jewish immigration to Palestine was well underway, driven by the anti-Semitism, discrimination, and pogroms that stateless Jews commonly experienced. Their idea of Zionism, to create a Jewish state for Jews everywhere, and continuing immigration soon encountered violence. Palestinian Arabs used terrorism in an effort to thwart the political goals of Zionists, and in 1936 the British also became targets of Palestinian terrorism. (At this point Britain introduced Defense Emergency Regulations, which the Israeli government continues to use to combat terrorism in the Occupied Territories.) Jews in Palestine began to organize, and some fought terror with terror. By the end of World War II, Britain confronted escalating terrorism in Palestine, as Arab and Jewish nationalist aspirations continued to clash. In 1946, Jewish terrorists bombed British headquarters; too weak to manage its violence-ridden mandated areas, Britain decided to leave Palestine to the supervision of the United Nations. The United Nations drew up a plan in 1947 to partition the area into separate states for Jews and Palestinians, but when British troops pulled out in 1948 the new state of Israel found itself under attack by its Arab neighbors. Jews successfully defended and enlarged the territory of Israel, and three-quarters of a million Palestinians fled to refugee camps in neighboring states. Over one hundred thousand Palestinians remained to become Israeli citizens.

From 1949 to 1967, Israel's terrorism problem stemmed from Palestinian *fedayeen* infiltrating over the 1949 armistice lines drawn between Israel and surrounding Arab states. The West Bank of the Jordan River (under Jordanian control since 1948) and the Gaza Strip (under Egyptian authority) were the primary sources of *fedayeen* attacks on Israelis. The Six-Day War of June 5–10, 1967, changed the nature of Israel's terrorism problem and created a very difficult set of new problems for the democratic government. Israel secured its borders in the 1967 war, taking control of the West Bank of the Jordan River, the Gaza Strip, the Golan Heights, and the eastern section of Jerusalem. The sites from which Palestinians had launched terrorist attacks on Israelis were now occupied by the Israeli Defense Forces (IDF). The territorial control brought Israel more secure borders but also approximately a million Palestinians, who represented an internal security threat of terrorism. Israel's response to Palestinian terrorism in the Occupied Territories is considered below, from the perspective of an observation made by Chaim Weizmann (first president of Israel) that the world would judge Zionists by their treatment of the Palestinians.

Israeli Counterterrorism Policies. Unlike West Germany and the United States, Israel's terrorism problem in the Occupied Territories was not the result of a student and civil rights movement or anti-Vietnam protests. Like Great Britain a half century earlier in Northern Ireland, Israel in 1967 found itself governing a hostile population with growing nationalist aspirations. (Israeli polls repeatedly show that over 90 percent of the Palestinians in Israel proper and the Occupied Territories acknowledge the Palestine Liberation Organization as their rightful representative[45] and desire a Palestinian state.) From 1967 to 1970, Palestinians operating from Jordan and in the Occupied Territories conducted a campaign of terrorist attacks on Israeli targets. IDF personnel were ambushed, and numerous civilian targets (supermarkets, schools, settlements, banks) were bombed or attacked. During this period, Israel put together an integrated set of countermeasures to deal with terrorism. First, the Israeli's set out their goals:

1. To minimize the actual damage terrorist attacks inflict, especially human casualties,
2. To destroy or reduce terrorists' resources,
3. To reduce the likelihood of future terrorist attacks.[46]

Next, Israel began integrating a system of four types of countermeasures:

1. Counterforce measures,
2. Measures to impede terrorists,
3. Passive defenses,
4. Punishments and reprisals.[47]

Counterforce measures include covert operations against Palestinian terrorist leaders and groups; and overt military force (air strikes; artillery, naval and infantry operations) to engage and destroy Palestinian attacks. To impede terrorist attacks, the Israelis gather intelligence and employ counterforce measures in addition to border and road patrols, and training bomb disposal squads. Passive defense measures include the construction of bomb shelters and border security systems (fences, roads, motion detectors). The fourth leg of the Israeli policy to counter terrorism involves the punishment of terrorists and those who aid and abet their attacks. It is primarily in this area that Israeli actions have received the greatest criticism, particularly concerning the violation of human rights in the Occupied Territories. Israel first was criticized for its counterterror policies by the international community in 1968, after an Israeli attack on the Beirut airport (thirteen Arab jetliners were destroyed); the raid came in retaliation against Palestinian attacks launched from southern Lebanon. (The IDF would invade this area in 1978 and 1982 in further attempts to root out terrorist bases.) Shortly thereafter, retaliatory raids would be launched against Jordanian territory from which Palestinians were conducting attacks. In 1970, Jordan's King Hussein engaged the Palestinians, who had triggered Israeli reprisals, and expelled them from Jordan. This marked the end of Palestinian operations from Jordanian territory against Israeli targets. As the raids from outside Israel diminished, terrorism in the West Bank and Gaza Strip increased.

In November 1968, the United Nations expressed its concern for Palestinians by establishing the U.N. Special Committee to Investigate Israeli Practices Affecting the Human Rights of the Population of the Occupied Territories. Sri Lanka, Somalia, and Yugoslavia were asked to oversee the committee, although none had diplomatic relations with Israel. The committee began to report complaints of collective punishment—(prolonged curfew, demolition of homes)—and other human rights abuses in Gaza in 1969. Reports since then have cited alleged torture in the Occupied Territories as part of Israeli counterterror measures. The more impartial and less hostile Amnesty International first cited charges by Palestinians in 1970 that detainees were tortured in the Occupied Territories. Since that time, criticism of Israel has revolved around two counterterror measures frequently employed in the Occupied Territories: (1) administrative detention (to prevent or impede terrorist activity) and (2) administrative punishment.

Administrative Detention. Administrative detention can be used to impede or punish terrorists, by detaining potential or suspected terrorists and also those who assist them. Administrative detention is authorized under the Defense Emergency Regulations (DER), a legacy of the British mandate that Israel has incorporated into its legal system. (DER restrictions on Jewish immigration and land purchases have been dropped.) The DER were used by the British to counter Palestinian terrorism in the 1936–1939 rebellion and later Jewish terrorism 1945–1948 by groups such as the Stern Gang and Menachem Begin's *Irgun Zvai Leumi*. (The *Irgun* had been created in 1935 as the military arm of the radical Zionist Revisionist Party, and was responsible for the 1946 bombing of the King David Hotel, British headquarters in Jerusalem.) The Defense Emergency Regulations authorized the British army (1) to confiscate or destroy private property, (2) to restrict access to property, (3) to censor all published material, (4) to restrict movement in or out of any area, (5) to deport terrorists, and (6) to detain suspected terrorists *indefinitely*. The Israeli military governor in the Occupied Territories uses the DER to authorize the controversial counterterror measure of administrative detention.

In 1967, over two thousand[48] Palestinians in the Occupied Territories were detained, declining to 1,131[49] detainees in 1970, 560[50] in 1971, and only forty[51] by 1976. In 1980, the practice of administrative detention fell into disuse but was reintroduced in 1984, when 473[52] Palestinians were again detained. Israel's harshest critics allege that administrative detention, in which a suspect can be held up to eighteen days incommunicado, has three purposes:

1. To gather intelligence, by torture if necessary,
2. To punish outspoken or uncooperative Palestinians, and
3. To detain those who threaten the Israeli presence.[53]

Incommunicado detention, its potential for abuse and subsequent allegations of torture were cited by Amnesty International in its 1981 report. AI expressed its concerns over the lack of effective safeguards to protect those under detention from ill-treatment. The same conditions had been noted earlier by the *London Sunday Times* Insight team, which went to the West Bank and Gaza Strip in 1977 to investigate allegations of torture by detainees. The *Times* report concluded that security and intelligence services did mistreat detainees and that six torture centers (in Nablus, Ramallah, Hebron, Gaza, Jerusalem, and a secret intelligence compound) were used for interrogation. The torture ranged from crude beatings to sophisticated electric-shock treatments. The Israeli government vigorously denounced the *Times* report, and the *Times* subsequently retracted its accusation that torture was systematically authorized at the highest levels of government. Neither the *Times* nor AI nor the U.N. Special Committee, however, have withdrawn their expressed concerns over the policy of administrative detention, per se, with its potential for abuse. The personal testimonials of mistreatment and torture continue, which the Israeli government explains are attempts by Palestinians to cover up their cooperation with the authorities, for they fear retribution from the PLO if they do not report being tortured while in custody. Each year, the United Nations Special Committee catalogs the statements of detainees who allege they were tortured to force confessions or to encourage them to emigrate. The Israeli government does not reply directly to the U.N. reports, but insists that medical exams before and after detention disprove the data collected by the United Nations.

The Israeli position on administrative detention, which it insists is a highly effective counterterror measure, was hurt by the *Shin Bet* (Israeli domestic intelligence) scandal in 1984. That year, two Palestinians who had hijacked an Israeli bus were captured and later died while in the custody of *Shin Bet* personnel. This incident renewed interest in administrative detention and abuses that may occur when a detainee is held without any outside contacts. (The Israelis usually permit visits by the International Committee of the Red Cross after fourteen days.) Amnesty International continues to point out its concern that better safeguards for prisoners and Israel's reputation should be added to the current practice of administrative detention. Preventive detention, as some Israelis call it, has created problems similar to those encountered by the British with their policy of internment in Northern Ireland: allegations of abuse and torture and accusations that detention is used to harass certain groups and to gather intelligence. Despite all the negative publicity surrounding the measure, Israel appears likely to continue its policy of administrative detention of Palestinians suspected of terrorism in the Occupied Territories.

Administrative Punishment. Israel has a well-known policy of retribution or reprisal against those who attack Israelis. After the 1972 massacre of Israeli athletes at the Olympic Games, Prime Minister Golda Meir authorized retaliatory attacks on Palestinian leaders. A unit from MOSSAD (Israeli intelligence) called *Mivtzan Elohim*, the "Wrath of God," targeted the heads of "Black September" and the PFLP for assassinations, which were carried out in Beirut, Paris, Rome, and Madrid. In the 1980s, attacks on Israelis typically have been followed by Israeli air strikes on the Palestinian camps or bases in Lebanon from which they originate. When terrorism occurs inside Israel or the Occupied Territories, a policy known as administrative punishment may be employed. Designed to punish terrorists and those who help them, as well as to deter future terrorism, administrative punishment is authorized under the DER and can take many forms.

As catalogued by U.N. reports and Amnesty International, administrative or "collective" punishment may include imposing curfews, closing shops and universities, interrupting electricity and telephone service to areas, searching large areas house-to-house, or deporting town mayors.[54] The strategy is to punish the entire community where terrorism has occurred and thereby undermine the support and resources terrorists might draw on for future attacks. The most sensational method of reprisal used in "administrative punishment" in the Occupied Territories involves the dynamiting or bulldozing of houses or buildings where suspected terrorists have stayed. In *Human Rights in the Administered Territories* (1978), a document published by the Embassy of Israel in Washington, D.C., the Israeli government states that the "demolition of homes, in circumstances where they were used to shelter terrorists is, in context, the most lenient as well as expedient of remedies."[55] The *Sunday Times* reported in 1977 that 16,212[56] homes had been destroyed by the government since 1967, although the International Committee of the Red Cross reported that 1,224[57] buildings were sealed or demolished during that period. The practice is a powerful, visual statement of punishment that attracts sensational attention, and is again in wide use, according to former deputy mayor of Jerusalem, Meron Benvenisti. In the 1986 update of the West Bank Data Project, Benvenisti disputes the government's claim that demolitions take place only after legal proceedings have established that a terrorist occupied a given home or building.

In 1984–85 the authorities made wide use of this punitive measure against security offenders. Demolition or sealing of houses precedes legal proceedings, and is considered a form of deterrent and collective punishment, since it affects the suspect's extended family residing in the house itself. The residents are not entitled to any compensation.[58]

The Occupied Territories present several thorny problems for an Israeli state that values its security as well as democratic values and human rights. The West Bank, which the Israelis now call Judea and Samaria, and the Gaza Strip hold territory that offers better security for Israel's borders but also hold a Palestinian population hostile to Israeli rule. Israel's counterterror policies in the Occupied Territories have made it the subject of numerous investigations and negative publicity. Israel has been accused of violating the Universal Declaration of Human Rights, including

Article 3: Everyone has the right to life, liberty and the security of person.

Article 5: No one shall be subjected to torture or to cruel, inhuman or degrading treatment or punishment.

Article 9: No one shall be subjected to arbitrary arrest, detention or exile.

Article 13.1: Everyone has the right to freedom of movement and residence within the borders of each state.

Article 17.2: No one shall be deprived of his property.

Because of the military occupation status under which the Occupied Territories exist, the Fourth Geneva Convention for the Protection of Civilian Persons in Time of War (1949) may be a more appropriate standard for evaluating Israel's policies. Under the Fourth Geneva Convention's provisions, however, Israel also has been accused of violations, citing article 53, which prohibits the destruction of private property, except where rendered absolutely necessary by military operations. Articles 27, 31, and 32 prohibit torture, mistreatment, and degrading punishment; these articles are also invoked by investigations that have alleged torture and mistreatment of detainees in the Occupied Territories. Article 78 of the Convention does permit the arrest and internment of individuals suspected of posing immediate threats to security. In reply to its critics, the Israeli government cites the Defense Emergency Regulations and the extraordinary threat terrorism poses in the Occupied Territories, and denies the abuses reported by the U.N. Special Committee, the *Sunday Times* and Amnesty International.

In addition to its hard line with terrorists, most notably reprisals and detention, Israel's counterterror repertoire includes several organizations specializing in the prevention and management of terrorism—that is, *Shin Bet* (*Sherut Habitachon*), which oversees intelligence and security in the Occupied Territories; *Sayaret Matkal*, the General Staff Reconnaissance Unit that specializes in counterterrorist operations such as the 1976 Entebbe rescue; MOSSAD, Israeli intelligence, which wages a covert war against the PLO; and LATAM, a Special Task Force Authority. The combination of the DER, the large, integrated system of countermeasures, and over a million Palestinians in the Occupied Territories has produced an environment in which terrorism threatens Israeli security and conterterrorism puts human rights and democratic values at risk. For Israel, more than any other liberal democracy, responding to terrorism requires a difficult balancing of values. For other liberal democracies, Israel's experiences hold valuable lessons on the costs and benefits of counterterrorism.

Summary

Democratic values are at risk when terrorism poses a threat to national security. In the Federal Republic of Germany, the news media cooperate with the government to blackout the publicity terrorists try to generate. In Northern Ireland, the British government confronts evidence that detainees have been tortured. In the United States, congressional investigations revealed numerous and systematic abuses of civil rights by the intelligence community in the 1960s and 1970s. And in the Occupied Territories, Israel again encounters both domestic and international criticism of its counterterrorism policies, which include curfews and the demolition of homes (collective punishment); deportation of Palestinians suspected of terrorism; and incommunicado administrative detention that often is followed by allegations of torture. The openness (free speech, freedom of movement and association) and the sensitivity of democratic states to public opinion produce a situation in which democratic values may be sacrificed for national security against terrorism. Even when terrorist groups fail in their long-term goals, over the short run they often succeed in undermining or weakening the essence of democracy: civil liberties. Terrorism is truly a double-edged sword threatening democracies like the Federal Republic of Germany, the United Kingdom, Israel, and the United States. Finding the means to counter terrorism without undermining democracy in the process of defending it remains the central challenge.

9
Terrorism, International Law, and International Organizations

> The purposes of the United Nations are: 1. To maintain international peace and security, and to that end: to take effective collective measures for the prevention and removal of threats to the peace, and for the suppression of acts of aggression or other breaches of the peace, and to bring about by peaceful means, and in conformity with the principles of justice and international law, adjustment or settlement of international disputes or situations which might lead to a breach of the peace. . . .
>
> —Charter of the United Nations, art. I.

International terrorism crosses national borders, targets citizens of many nations and exploits the technology of international travel and communication. Terrorists have targeted the Olympic Games (Munich 1972), diplomats, embassies, and international aviation. This chapter examines the responses of the international community to terrorism. The treatment of terrorism under international law and the key legal concepts applied to terrorism will be reviewed, including the definition of terrorism by the League of Nations (1937) and current efforts to define terrorism by the International Law Commission. Then the different types of responses that the international community has made to the problem of terrorism will be reviewed on four different levels:

1. Universal organization,
2. Multilateral organizations,
3. Bilateral agreements,
4. Unilateral action.

Terrorism and International Law

The community of nations has long recognized the danger of political violence and terrorism, and many laws and treaties have been written in efforts to cope with these problems. Terrorism also has required special legal treatment by states. Its political nature has led many states to provide terrorists with protection from extradition, and the "irregular" character of terrorist violence has made the law of armed conflicts appear inappropriate to the management of terrorism. The oldest legal principle used to deal with terrorism—*aut dedere, aut judicare* ("either extradite or prosecute")—was developed by Hugo Grotius in *De Jure Belli ac Pacis* (1624) (*On the Laws of War and Peace*), and appears in almost every international treaty or convention dealing with terrorism. The "political offense exception" to the prosecution or extradition of terrorists is a more recent development, first established in France by the Jacobean Constitution of 1793. The French Revolution began a long tradition in that country of granting asylum to foreigners who were fighting for liberty. In 1833 the Belgians followed the French example, enacting a law that fugitives would not be prosecuted or punished for any political offense, and many states followed their example. The tension between the legal principles "extradite or prosecute" and the "political offense exception" is one source of the weakness in efforts to apply international law to the prevention and punishment of terrorism.

The waves of terrorist bombings and assassinations across Europe in the late 1800s and early 1900s made the problem more visible and acute. The international community, however, had to wait until the end of World War I and the creation of the League of Nations before a cooperative international effort to punish and prevent terrorism could begin. The Convention of the League of Nations (Geneva, November 16, 1927) defined terrorism as activity that included

Efforts to force changes in government;

Disruption of public services or enterprises;

Poisoning of international relations;

Assassination attempts against heads of state or government representatives;

Destruction of public buildings, utilities, and communication;

Provocation of epidemics;

Pollution of food or water.[1]

(The convention never went into effect.)

Throughout the 1930s a series of six conferences were held in Europe by the Bureau for the Unification of Criminal Law, and three of the six meetings focused on terrorism. Many resolutions were passed, and a general theme treating terrorism as a threat to "collective security" emerged. In

1934, the League of Nations Council unanimously passed a resolution that "it is the duty of every State neither to encourage nor tolerate on its territory any terrorist activity with a political purpose." The Council further required that "every State must do all in its power to prevent and repress acts of this nature and must for this purpose lend its assistance to governments which request it" (December 10, 1934). The assassination of Yugoslavia's King Alexander at the hands of a Yugoslav refugee operating out of Hungary had brought the issue of terrorism before the League of Nations, but the Council went beyond the 1934 resolution. A committee was appointed to investigate terrorism, and the result of its work was the Convention for the Prevention and Punishment of Terrorism (adopted November 16, 1937, in Geneva). Although the convention never went into effect, it did establish two important precedents in the legal approach to terrorism. First, the convention affirmed that under international law and the League's charter states were obliged to prevent or punish acts of terrorism against other states that originated in their territory. Second, the convention set up an International Criminal Court and gave it jurisdiction to hear cases of alleged terrorism as defined by the Convention. World War II interrupted these efforts, which were not resumed until the 1950s under the auspices of the International Law Commission and the United Nations.

The International Law Commission drafted the Declaration on Rights and Duties of States for the new United Nations, and in that declaration (article 4) established the duty of every state "to refrain from fomenting civil strife in the territory of another State, and to prevent the organization within its territory of activities calculated to foment such civil strife." During this same period, the International Law Commission also prepared for the United Nations a Draft Code of Offenses Against the Peace and Security of Mankind. In article 2(6) of that code, international terrorism is described as the "undertaking or encouragement by the authorities of a State of terrorist activities in another State, or the toleration by the authorities of a State of organized activities calculated to carry out terrorist acts in another State."

International terrorism was then listed as an offense against the peace and security of mankind.[2] The work of the International Law Commission from 1947 to 1955 began to bear fruit in the U.N. General Assembly in 1957 with G.A. Resolution 1186(XII), which dealt with aggression and included terrorism. The General Assembly condemned the "sending by or on behalf of a State of armed bands, groups, irregulars or mercenaries, which carry out acts of armed force against another State. . . ."[3] The General Assembly reiterated its definition of and opposition to terrorism again in 1970 in G.A. Resolution 2625(XXIV)

Every State has the duty to refrain from organizing, instigating, assisting or participating in acts of civil strife or terrorist acts in another State. . . . Also, no State shall organize, assist, foment, finance, incite or tolerate subversive, terrorist or armed activities directed toward the violent overthrow of the regime of another State, or interfere in civil strife in another State.[4]

The apparent agreement on the issue of international terrorism at the United Nations would begin to disintegrate in 1972, when the United States introduced a Draft Convention for the Punishment of Certain Acts of International Terrorism following the massacre at the 1972 Olympic Games in Munich, Germany.

International Terrorism and the United Nations

U.N. Secretary-General Kurt Waldheim also had raised the issue of terrorism in the General Assembly, prior to the introduction of the United States Draft Convention for the Punishment of Certain Acts of International Terrorism in 1972. The failure of the efforts made by the Secretary-General and the U.S. delegation would reveal a deep split in United Nations opinion, centering around the distinction between "national wars of liberation" and "terrorism." The split is visible in the title of the first major investigation into terrorism by the U.N., Resolution 3034(XXVIII) (November 2, 1972):

Measures to prevent international terrorism which endangers or takes innocent human lives or jeopardizes fundamental freedoms, and study of the underlying causes of those forms of terrorism and acts of violence which lie in misery, frustration, grievance and despair and which cause some people to sacrifice human lives, including their own, in an attempt to effect radical change.

This resolution led to the creation of three committees to

1. Define terrorism,
2. Examine the causes of terrorism, and
3. Propose measures to prevent terrorism.

The split in the United Nations over these issues set one group of states (led by the United States and interested in preventing and punishing terrorism) against another group (led by Arab and African states and interested in the underlying causes of the violence). The committees did not agree on a definition of terrorism, but three decisions taken in the General Assembly in 1973 and 1974 reflect the controversy and disagreement generated in that body over the issue of terrorism:

1. The United States Draft Convention for the Punishment of Certain Acts of International Terrorism was rejected. The committees found that the United States was attempting to label the "legitimate struggle of peoples for national liberation" as terrorism. Resolution A/9890 was added to the committee's report, preserving the "right to self-determination, freedom and independence . . . particularly for people under colonial and racist regimes or other forms of alien domination . . . the right of these people to struggle to that end and to seek and receive support. . . ."

2. The General Assembly voted to grant "permanent observer status" to a delegation representing the Palestinian people (1974).

3. The General Assembly approved the Convention on the Prevention and Punishment of Crimes against Internationally Protected Persons, including Diplomatic Agents (1974). This convention covers acts of kidnapping, assault, or murder on protected persons; attacks on premises or transportation facilities used by protected persons; and threats of any such attacks. The convention calls for the coordination of states' laws against these acts and for cooperation among states to prevent and punish such attacks.

The actions taken by the General Assembly in this period reflected deep disagreement over the concept of "justifiable" political violence. The General Assembly's only action—the consensus adoption of the Convention on the Prevention and Punishment of Crimes against Internationally Protected Persons, including Diplomatic Agents—merely reconfirmed the oldest and most widely recognized principle of international diplomacy, i.e., the inviolability of diplomats and embassies. The General Assembly, as noted above, passed the convention by a consensus vote, and fewer than sixty members actually have ratified it. Ratification obligates a state to extradite or prosecute individuals accused of violations of the convention, and because it has not been widely ratified, enforcement of the convention has been undermined. Although the General Assembly has endorsed the concept of the inviolability of diplomats, the actual measures taken by it to protect diplomatic personnel and facilities have been modest, at best.

The General Assembly saw no further progress on this issue until 1979, when the United States Embassy in Tehran, Iran, was occupied in November and American personnel were held hostage. In December, the General Assembly passed Resolution 34/145, the Convention against the Taking of Hostages. The following year it adopted a Resolution on Measures to Enhance the Protection, Security, and Safety of Diplomatic and Consular

Missions and Representatives. These resolutions require the extradition or prosecution of persons alleged to have taken hostages, and no "political offense exception" is allowed. Ratification of these measures has been spotty, indicating that although the General Assembly appreciates the importance of diplomatic inviolability, it cannot agree on how to compel states to provide adequate protection to diplomats. Because of the symbolic value attached to diplomatic missions and personnel, and the inability of the United Nations to enforce host states' obligation to protect them, individual states have assumed the responsibility of protecting their diplomats and facilities overseas. The U.S. government, for example, appropriated over $1 billion in 1984 to improve the physical security of its embassies and to train staff to avoid terrorist attacks abroad.

Other organs of the United Nations also took action during the 1979–1981 occupation of the U.S. embassy and the detention of fifty four U.S. American hostages in Tehran. The Security Council passed a resolution calling for the immediate release of the hostages, but the Soviet Union vetoed a measure to impose economic sanctions against Iran. The International Court of Justice held that Iran had incurred international liability for the breach of diplomatic inviolability and could be sued by the United States. The office of the General-Secretary assisted in the mediation efforts, as well.

Overall, the United Nations General Assembly and Security Council have been immobilized by political differences concerning terrorism and struggles for national liberation. The site of the United Nations' longest and possibly most effective efforts to combat international terrorism has been the U.N.'s International Civil Aviation Organization (ICAO).

ICAO and Conventions to Protect International Aviation

The more technical issues of protecting international airline traffic and airports from terrorist attacks have been discussed in the International Civil Aviation Organization. Three agreements have emerged that, together with technical improvements in security (metal detectors, x-ray devices) have greatly reduced terrorist attacks on civil aviation. The three agreements include

1. The Tokyo Convention on Offenses and Certain Other Acts Committed on Board Aircraft (1963),
2. The Hague Convention for the Suppression of Unlawful Seizure of Aircraft (1970),

3. The Montreal Convention for the Suppression of Unlawful Acts against the Safety of Civil Aviation (1971).

The Tokyo Convention dates back to 1963 when preliminary discussions about illegal diversion of international air traffic took place. The convention was ratified in 1969 after a significant increase in hijackings (or skyjackings) took place:[5]

Year	Hijackings
1961	11
1962	4
1963	1
1964	2
1965	5
1966	4
1967	7
1968	35
1969	89
1970	88
1971	61
1972	65
1973	23
1974	27
1975	26
1976	22

The Tokyo Convention required all ratifying states promptly to repatriate hijacked airliners and passengers, but the convention did not invoke the principle of "either extradite or prosecute." That step was taken in the Hague Convention (1970), which obliged all ratifying states to extradite hijackers or prosecute them on domestic criminal charges. The Hague Convention did allow states to maintain the "political offense exception," preserving their right to grant asylum to hijackers. The Montreal Convention the next year expanded the scope of offenses to include terrorist attacks on grounded aircraft and airport facilities.

Over one hundred nations are party to each of these conventions. Unfortunately, the enforcement mechanisms are absent or very weak, as demonstrated by Uganda's assistance to hijackers in the 1976 Entebbe episode, despite that nation's ratification of the conventions. Uganda was never punished or censured for its aid to the hijackers. Many states still refuse to ratify the agreements, and the "political offense exception" inhibits the extradition of most of the hijackers. (States tend to expel hijackers rather than extradite them.) The number of hijackings has stabilized at around thirty per year, worldwide.[6]

Year	Hijackings
1977	32
1978	31
1979	27
1980	41
1981	32
1982	32

Many experts attribute the decline in hijackings to improved airport security practices and equipment. The use of metal detectors and the inspection of carry-on baggage has reduced the number of weapons reaching aircraft, and the segregation of passengers prior to boarding enables security teams to scrutinize suspicious customers before international flights.

ICAO support and sponsorship of international conventions to prevent and punish terrorist attacks on aviation have been the most visible efforts made by the international community to deal with this threat to a collective concern—i.e., safe, international civil aviation. These efforts have been undermined by states that refuse to ratify, by the lack of an enforcement convention, and by states that insist that they reserve the right to grant "political exceptions" to prosecution and/or extradition.

Terrorism and Multilateral Organizations: The European Convention on the Suppression of Terrorism and the Organization of American States (OAS) Conventions on Terrorism

Regional, multilateral organizations have also attempted to take collective action to prevent and punish terrorism. These organizations have more homogenous membership than the politically divided United Nations, but multilateral agreements to counter terrorism also suffer many of the same problems encountered by U.N. efforts in this area (political offense exception, lack of enforcement, lack of signatories). Seven multilateral organizations have worked on terrorism agreements, two of which will be discussed next, including the Council of Europe's Convention on the Suppression of Terrorism and the Organization of American States (OAS) agreements on terrorism and hostage taking.

There now exist more than a dozen multilateral agreements and conventions dealing with terrorism made by a variety of organizations. The Nordic League (Norway, Sweden, Denmark, Iceland, and Finland) has a strong extradition treaty dating to 1962. The British Commonwealth countries, the Arab League, the Benelux countries, the European Community, the Organization of American States, and the Organization Communale Africaine at Malgache also have extradition agreements, and several cooperate in areas including narcotics and terrorism. The European and OAS Conventions on Terrorism have gone furthest in efforts to prevent and punish terrorism.

The European Convention on the Suppression of Terrorism (ECST) (1978)

Three terrorist acts in Europe in the 1970s laid the groundwork for the European Convention on the Suppression of Terrorism (ECST), sponsored by the Council of Europe. The attack on Israeli athletes in Munich during the 1972 Olympics, the 1977 kidnapping and murder of German industrialist Hans Martin Schleyer, and the 1978 abduction and assassination of former Italian Prime Minister Aldo Moro prompted the Council of Europe to conclude an agreement with five salient features:

1. The ECST is, above all else, a cooperative effort to mesh extradition policies and laws of the signatories in order to enhance the prosecution of terrorists.
2. The ECST avoids defining terrorism.
3. The ECST reaffirms the principle of *aut dedere aut judicare* ("either extradite or prosecute").
4. The ECST does not attempt to establish an international court for prosecuting terrorists.
5. The ECST attempts to eliminate the "political offense exception," which states use to avoid extraditing or prosecuting terrorists. Hijackings, hostage-taking, and attacks on "protected persons" are not considered "political offenses." The ECST, however, allows signatories to "register a reservation," which then permits a state to deny a request for extradition. The "reservation" clause thereby preserves the states' prerogative to grant asylum to terrorists or "political offenders."

The ECST is not considered "successful" in reducing terrorism, but it is noteworthy for highlighting the difficulties that plague multilateral efforts against terrorism. Although many states (Austria, Cyprus, Denmark, Federal Republic of Germany, Iceland, the United Kingdom, Norway, Spain, Sweden) have ratified the European Convention, two important states have not. France and Ireland are not parties to the ECST, primarily due to objections over the convention's infringement on states' rights to grant asylum and deny extradition. The importance given by these countries to the distinction between "political offenses" (that merit asylum) and political terrorism is significant. The ECST does not attempt to define terrorism, and the debate continues over what constitutes justifiable political violence.

Organization of American States (OAS) Conventions on Terrorism

Terrorist activity in South America in the 1960s had brought the need for multilateral cooperation before the Organization of American States. The OAS passed Resolution AB/Res. 4 (I-E/70) in 1970, by which the member states agreed

1. To condemn strongly, as crimes against humanity, acts of terrorism and especially the kidnapping of persons and extortion in connection with that crime,
2. To condemn such acts, when perpetrated against representatives of foreign states, as violations not only of human rights but also of the norms that govern international relations,
3. To declare that these acts constitute serious crimes,
4. To request the governments of the member states to facilitate the exchange of information that will help in the prevention and punishment of crimes of this kind.

The result of the resolution was a Convention to Prevent and Punish the Acts of Terrorism Taking the Forms of Crimes against Persons and Related Extortion That Are of International Significance (1971). Twenty-two governments attended the OAS conference that drafted the convention, but fewer than one-third have ratified it. The convention made several early contributions to the multilateral approach to terrorism, (1) confirming the principle *aut dedere, aut judicare* and (2) subjecting crimes against diplomats to "universal jurisdiction." The latter empowers any member state to exercise criminal jurisdiction over a terrorist attack on protected persons, no matter where the attack occurred. The weaknesses of the convention are familiar: it has been ratified by only six states, and it preserves the right of states to grant asylum. Like the United Nations convention, OAS efforts to safeguard diplomatic personnel also set no standards for security practices.

In 1981, the OAS again took up the issue of terrorism—specifically, the problem of extradition. The result was the OAS Inter-American Convention on Extradition, which attempts to strip hijacking, hostage-taking, and attacks on protected persons of the "political offense exception," and subsequently to deprive terrorists of sanctuary or asylum. The 1981 convention also has not been widely ratified. Improved security practices protecting airline traffic and diplomatic personnel may have weakened the United States' efforts to encourage other OAS members to ratify the convention.

Bilateral Cooperation on Terrorism

The political difficulties confronted by a universal organization such as the United Nations in its struggle to define and combat terrorism, or the similar problems encountered by multilateral organizations, can often be avoided when two nations undertake bilateral solutions to a mutual terrorism problem. Agreements to punish hijackers and/or guarantee the prompt return of passengers and aircraft are the most common type of bilateral arrangements involving terrorism. The Soviet Union, for example, has such agreements with Afghanistan, Finland, and Iran. Cuba has hijacking agreements with the United States, Venezuela, Mexico, and Colombia.

The Cuban-American Memorandum of Understanding on Hijacking of Aircraft and Vessels and Other Offenses (1973) demonstrates how effectively bilateral agreements can reduce terrorist hijackings, even when the states involved are unfriendly and do not maintain full diplomatic relations. The Cuban-American agreement (denounced by Fidel Castro in 1976 but, nonetheless, still adhered to in practice) is possibly the toughest terrorism agreement in existence between two states. This bilateral arrangement provides

1. That hijackers be extradited or put on trial;
2. That neither party allow its territory to be used as a base of operations against the territory or property of the other state; and
3. That asylum can be granted only if the hijacking involved no ransom demands and caused no injuries to any passengers.

The United States was satisfied with Cuban compliance with the spirit and letter of the agreement, particularly Cuba's demonstration of its willingness to convict and imprison hijackers. Explaining the decline in hijackings from the United States to Cuba, however, must also take into account technological improvements in airline security. The figures below indicate that hijackings from the United States to Cuba actually began to decline prior to the 1973 agreement:

| | Hijackings |
Year	(United States to Cuba)
1966	0
1967	1
1968	14
1969	20
1970	13
1971	5
1972	6
1973	1
1974	1
1975	1

The United States has also concluded a Supplemental Treaty Concerning the Extradition Treaty between the Government of the United States of America and the Government of the United Kingdom of Great Britain and Northern Ireland. This bilateral agreement does not involve hijacking but addresses the Reagan administration's concern that Provisional Irish Republican Army members avoid extradition and that "the United States has become a sanctuary for terrorist murderers."[8] The Supplemental Treaty is intended to remove the "political offense exception" when violent crimes are involved and also to remove the power to refuse extradition from the hands of U.S. magistrates. (Since 1979, U.S. judges have rejected four British requests to extradite Provisional IRA fugitives on the basis of the "political offense exception.") The U.S. government encountered opposition in the ratification process from Irish-American organizations and Senators sympathetic to the Irish "national liberation" cause. Even in bilateral agreements, defining terrorism and distinguishing it from struggles for national liberation create difficulties for governments taking a legalistic approach to the problem of terrorism.

Unilateral Responses to Terrorism

When states resort to "self-help" measures to deal with problems of international terrorism, they often have exhausted the more orthodox international legal remedies or failed to obtain assistance from international organizations. This was the case in the hijacking in which Israelis were held hostage at Entebbe in 1976 and also the scenario involving U.S. military intervention in Iran in 1980 and Libya in 1986.

In June 1976, an Air France jet was hijacked from Athens by Palestinians (members of the Popular Front for the Liberation of Palestine). The plane was flown to Uganda, where the government allowed more Palestinians to board the plane. Ninety-six Israelis were held hostage, and the

Israeli government decided to dispatch three planeloads of commandos to rescue its citizens after Ugandan President Idi Amin announced that he supported the PFLP and its demands for the release of fifty three prisoners. The raid was stunningly successful: one Israeli commando died, four hostages were lost, and all the hijackers were killed. The Ugandan government was embarrassed and furiously demanded that the U.N. Security Council punish Israel for its "act of aggression." The Security Council declined. The example set by Israel's self-reliant and forceful solution to the Entebbe situation left a vivid impression. The German GSG-9 Commando team conducted a similar rescue mission one year later in Mogadishu, Somalia, and many Western nations began training teams modeled after the Israeli commandos and German GSG-9 to deal with hostage-taking crises.

In November 1979, the United States embassy in Tehran was overrun and occupied, with fifty four Americans held hostage (black and female staff members were sent home in the first weeks of the crisis). The United States obtained a unanimous Security Council motion calling for the immediate release of all Americans, and the World Court made similar demands on Iran. Nevertheless, the Iranian government did not order the occupiers of the embassy to release the Americans. Frustrated by the failure of its efforts to put legal, multilateral, and economic pressure on Iran, the U.S. government attempted a rescue of the hostages in April 1980 that was aborted in the Iranian desert. The United States was embarrassed and returned to negotiating for the hostages' release. Over $40 billion in Iranian assets had been frozen in U.S. banks and financial institutions, leading many critics to argue that the United States had not chosen the "course of last resort" in the rescue mission but had succumbed to the precedent set by the Israelis' raid on Entebbe. Not wanting to appear impotent and frustrated by the process of dealing with a radical government in Tehran, U.S. President Jimmy Carter opted for unilateral action, which failed.

Carter's successor, President Ronald Reagan, also opted for unilateral action in the matter of Libyan involvement in terrorist attacks on U.S. servicemen in Germany. After a 1986 discotheque bombing in Berlin in which one American serviceman died and evidence later indicated Libyan involvement, President Reagan ordered a bombing attack on Libyan military facilities. United States efforts to impose economic sanctions had proven ineffective, and the U.N. General Assembly was disinclined to censure Libya's Muammar Kaddafi. The U.S. raid on Libya took place in April 1986, with British Prime Minister Thatcher allowing American F-111s to fly out of Lakenheath Air Base to join the attack. The F-111s targeted the home of Kaddafi, whom President Reagan had called "the mad dog of the Middle East." Twelve navy A-6s, operating from a carrier in the Mediterranean, were assigned to bomb an airfield and barracks. Kaddafi survived the raid and protested the "American aggression," while President Reagan declared that the United States had acted "in self-defense." The American raid was not completely unilateral, as the British government had allowed the use of Lakenheath Air Base in the mission. (The French government, however, had denied overflight permission, greatly increasing the length and risk of the F-111s' mission.) The success of the unilateral action has since been vigorously debated in the United States and in the international community.

Summary

The Ineffectiveness of International Organizations and Law in Combating Terrorism

Why have the multilateral efforts made by the United Nations and other regional organizations been so weak and ineffective? Why is international law not put to work to counter terrorism? The reasons for the ineffectual responses offered by the international community to terrorism's challenge are many and complex. A list of those reasons, as illustrated in the examples of the United Nations' multilateral, bilateral, and unilateral responses to terrorism, includes the following:

1. The United Nations has chosen to adopt a political approach to aggression and terrorism. The League of Nations' failure convinced many that a legal approach to these problems would not work. Legal systems require shared values, and those do not exist in sufficient measure at today's United Nations to support legal remedies to terrorism.

2. The members of the United Nations have shown repeatedly that they value their independence and sovereignty more than security from terrorism. The prerogative to grant asylum, for example, is something states refuse to give up despite the need to extradite and prosecute terrorists.

3. The United Nations has other built-in barriers to universal organizational cooperation on terrorism. Ideological differences lead different states to consider different actions as terroristic. Also, the interdependence between some states inhibits them from taking a strong position on terrorism. States that import large amounts of Middle East petroleum, for example, fear they cannot afford to comment on Palestinian terrorism.

4. The United Nations has inadequate peace-keeping capability to try to effect military solutions to terrorism.

5. International law also lacks a potent enforcement mechanism to prevent or punish international terrorism. (Again, this is the result of states' decisions to preserve their maximum autonomy.)

6. Multilateral and U.N. agreements usually fail to obtain unanimous approval, which undermines collective enforcement. States have different, frequently conflicting interests that they pursue and that may cause them to refuse to ratify terrorism conventions.

7. Bilateral and unilateral action also must be taken by governments. Bureaucratic responses are often halting and ineffective, e.g., U.S. efforts to extradite Provisional IRA fugitives or the 1980 rescue mission to Iran.

8. Within most organizations the debate between those interested in the causes of terrorism and others interested in punishing terrorists continues. This debate characterizes the confusion and difficulty organizations and states face in formulating a response to international terrorism.

9. The most effective response to terrorism comes from the targets, those who have the most to lose. Targets such as airlines, diplomats, and businesses have taken the quickest and, to date, most effective action to prevent further attacks. The action has been technical, not political, which may account for its speed. This reflects, perhaps, the opinion of the international community that it is not a target, per se, of terrorism.

Trends and Prospects in International Terrorism

Terrorism is one of the plagues of modern times. None of the many different sources of terrorism—desire for national liberation or radical change, the usefulness of terrorism in governance and foreign policy—are likely to diminish or disappear soon. Terrorism will remain part of post–World War II politics, and the United Nations and international law will continue to be ineffective tools to combat terrorism. The conflicting interests of nation-states will continue to make universal countermeasures impossible.

As the targets of terrorism improve their ability to prevent or manage terrorist attacks with rescue teams, technology and bi- or multilateral agreements, terrorists will adapt and find new, vulnerable areas to attack. Most prominent on the list of prospective targets are nuclear facilities, electric power plants, oil transport facilities, water supplies, biological and chemical weapons laboratories, and communications networks. For all the exotic and high technology weapons and targets available to terrorists, however, they have little reason to abandon the simple and readily available tools now at their disposal. Targets remain abundant and vulnerable, and the media continue to provide publicity when terrorists seek it. Terrorism promises to remain a difficult and persistent feature of international violence, with no remedies or fail-safe defenses yet on the horizon.

Appendix
Terrorist Groups

Argentina

Alianza Anticomunista Argentina (AAA) (Argentine Anticommunist Alliance)
Ejercito Revolucionario del Pueblo (ERP) (People's Revolutionary Army)
Montoneros

Belgium

CCC (Fighting Communist Cells)

Bolivia

Ejercito de la Liberacion Nacional (ELN) (National Liberation Army)
Esquadron de la Muerta (Death Squad)
Movimiento de la Izquierda Revolucionaria (MIR) (Movement of the Revolutionary Left)

Brazil

Ačao Libertadora Nacional (ALN) (National Liberation Action)

Canada

Front de Liberation du Quebec (FLQ) (Quebec Liberation Front)

Chile

Movimiento de la Izquierda Revolucionaria (MIR) (Movement of the Revolutionary Left)

Colombia

Movimiento de abril 19 (M19) (Movement of April 19)

Costa Rica

Fuerzas Armadas de Liberacion Nacional (FALN) (Armed Forces of National Liberation)

Cuba

Omega 7

Egypt

al Takfir Wal Higra (Atonement and Holy Flight)

El Salvador

Ejercito Revolucionario del Pueblo (ERP) (People's Revolutionary Army)
Esaquadron de la Muerta (Death Squad)
Farabundo Marti Fuerzas Populares de Liberacion Nacional (FMLN) (Farabundo Marti Popular Forces of National Liberation)
Organizacion Democratica Nacional (ORDEN) (National Democratic Organization)

France

Action Directe (AD) (Direct Action)
Corsican National Liberation Front (FLNC)
(Guadeloupe) Caribbean Revolutionary Alliance (ARC)
Front de Liberation de la Bretagne—Armée Revolutionnaire Bretonne (FLB-ARB) (Liberation Front of Brittany—Revolutionary Breton Army)

Germany (West)

Baader-Meinhof Gang, Rote Armee Fraktion (RAF) (Red Army Faction)
Bewegung 2 Juni (2nd June Movement)
Revolutionare Zellen (RZ) (Revolutionary Cells)
Rote Hilfe (Red Help)
Wehrsport Gruppe Hoffmann (Defense Sport Group)

Haiti

Tonton Macoutes

Honduras

MR 19
Mano Blanco (White Hand)

Greece

17 November

India

Dal Khalsa
Naxalites

Ireland

Irish National Liberation Army (INLA)
Irish Republican Army (IRA)
Provisional Irish Republican Army (PIRA)
Ulster Freedom Fighters (UFF)
Ulster Protestant Voulnteers (UPV)
Ulster Volunteer Force (UVF)

Israel

al Fatah
Democratic Front for the Liberation of Palestine (DFLP)
Popular Front for the Liberation of Palestine (PFLP)
Popular Front for the Liberation of Palestine—General Command
(PFLP-GC)
Saiqa
abu Nidal Group
Gush Emunim

Italy

Brigate Rosse (Red Brigades)
Nuclei Armati Rivoluzionari (NAR) (Armed Revolutionary Nuclei)

Japan

Sekigun (Japanese Red Army)

Lebanon

al Da'awa
Hezbollah
Islamic Amal
Islamic Jihad
Phalange

Netherlands

Dutch Red Help
Republik Malaku Selatan (Independent Republic of Molucca)

Nicaragua

Fuerzas Armadas Revolucionarias de Nicaragua (FARN) (Nicaraguan Armed Revolutionary Forces)
Fuerzas Democraticas de Nicaragua (FDN) (Democratic Forces of Nicaragua)
MISURASATA (Miskito, Sumu, and Rama Indian Movement)
Unidad Democratica Nacional (UDN) (Nicaraguan Democratic Union)
United Nicaraguan Opposition (UNO)

Peru

Frente Izquierdista Revolucionaria (FIR) (Revolutionary Leftist Front)
Movimiento de la Izquierda Revolucionaria (MIR) (Revolutionary Left Movement)
Sendero Luminoso (Shining Path)

Purtugal

PF25 (Popular Forces of April 25)

Spain

Euzkadi Ta Askatasuna (ETA) (Basque Homeland and Freedom)
Grupo de Resistencia Antifascista Primo de Octubre (GRAPO) (1st of October Anti-Fascist Resistance Group)
Guerrillos del Cristo Rey (Warriors of Christ the King)

Sri Lanka

Tamil Liberation Tigers

Turkey

Armenian Secret Army for the Liberation of Armenia (ASALA)
Dev Sol (Revolutionary Left)
Dev Yol (Revolutionary Path)
Grey Wolves
Kurdish Workers Party (PKK)
Turkish People's Liberation Army (TPLA)

United Kingdom

Animal Rights Militia
Cadwyr Cymru (CC)
(Keepers of Wales)
Mudiad Amddiffyn Cymru (MAC)
(Free Wales Army)

United States of America

Aryan Nations
Cross, Sword and Arm (CSA)
Ku Klux Klan (KKK)
National Socialist White People's Party
Posse Comitatus

Uruguay

Movimiento de Liberacion Nacional (MLN)
also known as the Tupamaros

Yugoslavia

Hrvatsko Revolucionarno Bratstvo (HRB) (Croatian Revolutionary Brotherhood)
Ustashe (Insurgents)

Notes

Chapter 1

1. Netanyahu, Benjamin, *Terrorism: How the West Can Win*. (New York: Farrar, Straus, Giroux, 1986), p.9.
2. Crenshaw, Martha, "How Terrorism Ends." Paper presented at the American Political Science Association, Chicago, IL., 1987, p.4.
3. Alex Schmid, *Political Terrorism: A Research Guide*. (New Brunswick, N.J.: Transaction, 1984).

Chapter 2

1. Josephus, Flavius, *Antiquities*, 18:23.
2. Avi-Yonah, M., *The Jews under Roman and Byzantine Rule* (New York: Schocken, 1984).
3. Josephus, Flavius, *The Great Roman-Jewish War: A.D. 66–70* (New York: Harper, 1960). sec. VII, ch. 8, no. 336.
4. *Ibid.*, sec. VII, ch. 8, no. 406.
5. Palmer, R. R., *Twelve Who Ruled: The Year of Terror in the French Revolution*. (New York: Atheneum, 1965), p.5.
6. Soboul, Albert, *The French Revolution 1787–1799* (New York: Vintage, 1975) p. 388.
7. *Ibid.*
8. Greer, Donald, *The Incidence of the Terror during the French Revolution: A Statistical Interpretation* (Goucester, Mass.: Peter Smith, 1966), p. 37.
9. Stewart, John Hall, *A Documentary Survey of the French Revolution* (New York: MacMillan, 1951), p. 479.
10. Soboul, p. 388.
11. *Ibid.*
12. *Ibid.*
13. Robespierre, M. Speech to the National Convention, Paris, February 5, 1794.

14. Mathews, Shailer, *The French Revolution: A Sketch* (New York: Longmans, Green, 1901), p. 256.

15. Stewart, p. 520.

16. Palmer, R. R., *Twelve Who Ruled: The Year of the Terror in the French Revolution* (New York: Atheneum, 1965).

17. Talmon, J. L., *The Origins of Totalitarian Democracy* (New York: Secker & Warburg, 1952).

18. Godwin, William, *An Inquiry Concerning Political Justice*, pp. 548–549, as cited in Paul Eltzbacher, *Anarchism* (London: Freedom Press, 1960), pp. 25–26.

19. Proudhon, Pierre Joseph, "What Is Property?" (New York: Humboldt Publishing Co., 1891).

20. Proudhon, Pierre Joseph, *Justice* (translated by New York: Humboldt Publishing Co., 1891), 3, 45.

21. Bakunin, Mikhail, quoted in Robert Hunter, *Violence and the Labor Movement* (New York: Arno, 1969), p. 6.

22. Bakunin, Mikhail, and Nechaev, S., *The Catechism of the Revolutionist* (1866), as quoted in Max Nomad, *Aspects of Revolt* (New York: Bookman, 1959), p. 166.

23. Carr, E. H., *The Romantic Exiles* (Boston: Beacon Press, 1933), p. 290.

24. Kropotkin, Peter, *Paroles d'un Revolté*, (Geneva, 1885), p. 285, as cited in Eltzbacher, p. 121.

25. Miller, Martin A., *Kropotkin* (Chicago: University of Chicago Press, 1976), citing Kropotkin in *Le Révolté* (Dec. 25, 1880).

26. Kropotkin, as quoted in Eltzbacher, p. 99.

27. *Ibid.*, p. 116.

28. Emile Henry, at his trial for the bombing of a Paris café (1894).

29. Barrows, Susanna, *Distorting Mirrors: Visions of the Crowd in Late Nineteenth Century France* (New Haven, Conn.: Yale University Press, 1981), p. 38.

30. Hunter, Robert, *Violence and the Labor Movement* (New York: Arno Press, 1969), p. 95.

31. Avrich, Paul, *The Russian Anarchists* (Princeton, N.J.: Princeton University Press, 1967), p. 60.

32. *Ibid.*, p. 64.

Chapter 3

1. Cronin, Sean, *Irish Nationalism* (New York: Continuum 1981), p. 131.

2. Hitler, Adolf, Public Speech, Berlin, Germany, 1939.

3. Rosie, George, *Directory of International Terror* (New York: Paragon House, 1986), p. 57.

4. Porter, Jack Nusan, ed., *Genocide and Human Rights* (New York: University Press of America, 1982), p. 105.

5. *Ibid.*, p. 99.

6. Turki, Fawaz, *The Disinherited, Journal of a Palestinian Exile* (New York: Modern Reader, 1972), p. 16.

7. Rosie, p. 114.

Chapter 4

1. Kuper, Leo, *Genocide: Its Political Use in the Twentieth Century* (New Haven: Yale University Press, 1982), p. 124.

2. *Ibid.*, p. 141.

3. Amnesty International, "Political Killings by Governments" (London: AI, 1983), p. 38.

4. *Ibid.*, p. 44.

5. *Ibid.*, p. 38.

6. Simpson, John and Jana Bennett, *The Disappeared and the Mothers of the Plaza* (New York: St. Martins Press, 1985), p. 76.

7. Simpson, John, and Jana Bennett, *The Disappeared and the Mothers of the Plaza* (New York: St. Martin's Press, 1985), p. 400.

8. *Ibid.*, p. 399.

9. *Ibid.*, p. 76.

10. *Ibid.*

11. *Ibid.*, p. 65.

12. *Ibid.*

13. *Ibid.*, p. 54.

14. *Ibid.*, p. 81.

15. *Ibid.*, p. 41.

16. Elena Bonner, et al., Open letter to Secretary Brezhnev, Moscow (July 1973).

17. Treadgold, Donald W., *Twentieth Century Russia*, 2d ed. (Chicago: Rand McNally, 1964), p. 11.

18. Adelman, Jonathon R., *Terror and Communist Politics* (Boulder, Colo.: Westview Press, 1984), p. 108.

19. Filatova, A. P., Jr., Interview in *The Lancet*, April 11, 1981, p. 822.

20. Bloch, Sidney, and Peter Reddaway, *Psychiatric Terror* (New York: Basic Books, 1977), p. 43.

21. Koryagin, Anatoly, "Unwilling Patients," *The Lancet* 1 (1981): 821.

Chapter 5

1. Dekmejian, R., *Islam on Revolution* (Syracuse, N.Y.: Syracuse University Press, 1985), p. 58.

2. Taheri, Amir, *The Spirit of Allah: Khomeini and the Islamic Revolution* (Bethesda, Md.: Adler & Adler, 1986), p. 32.

3. Rosie, George, *The Directory of International Terrorism* (New York: Paragon House, 1986), p. 248.

Chapter 6

1. Schmid, Alex P., and Janny deGraaf, *Violence as Communication* (London: Sage, 1982), p. 17.

2. Schmid and deGraaf, p. 32.

3. Times Mirror, *The People and the Press* (Los Angeles: Times Mirror, 1986), p. 11–12. (October 20, 1986): 72. Reprinted by permission.

4. Sommer, Michael, "Nation's Police Chiefs, Media Differ of Terrorism Coverage" (Northridge, Calif.: California State University, 1978).

5. *TV Guide* (February 23, 1985): 3.

6. Charles Krauthammer, *Harper's*. Copyright © 1984 by *Harpers Magazine*. All rights reserved. Reprinted from the October issue by special permission.

7. Morton Dean, Minneapolis *Star and Tribune* (July 14, 1985).

8. *More* (June 1977): p. 21.

9. Schlesinger, Philip, "The BBC and Northern Ireland," in Peter Taylor, ed., *The British Media and Ireland* (London: Constable, 1978).

Chapter 7

1. Cline, Ray, and Yonah Alexander, *Terrorism: The Soviet Connection* (New York: Crane and Russak, 1984), p. 6.

2. *Pravda*, June 6, 1972.

3. Goren, Roberta, *The Soviet Union and Terrorism* (London: Allen & Unwin, 1984), p. 138.

4. Sterling, Clair, "Terrorism: Tracing the International Network," *New York Times Magazine* (March 1, 1981): p. 19.

5. Luttwark, Edward, *The Grand Strategy of the Soviet Union* (New York: St. Martin's Press, 1983), p. 64.

6. LeMoyne, James, "The Guerrilla Network," *New York Times Magazine* (April 6, 1986): 20.

7. Stohl, Michael, "States, Terrorism and State Terrorism: The Role of the Superpowers," Symposium on International Terrorism, Defense Intelligence Agency, Washington, D.C., 1985.

8. Cockburn, Alexander, "Beat the Devil: The CIA's Master Plan," *The Nation* (August 17, 24, 1985): p. 103.

9. General L. L. Lemnitzer, Chairman, Joint Chief of Staff, Memo for the Special Assistant to the President for National Security Affairs, in "A Summary of U.S. Military Counter-Insurgency Accomplishments since January 1, 1961" (July 17, 1962).

10. *Psychological Operations in Guerrilla Warfare* (New York: Random House, 1985), p. 57.

11. U.S. Department of the Army, Army Concept Team, Vietnam, "Employment of a Special Forces Group" (April 20, 1966).

12. McClintock, Michael, *The American Connection*, vol. 1 (London: Zed Books, 1985), p. 45.

13. *Ibid.*, p. 46.

14. Lipsman, Samuel, and Edward Doyle, *Fighting for Time* (Boston: Boston, 1983), p. 80.

15. Marchetti, Victor, and John D. Marks, *The CIA and the Cult of Intelligence* (New York: Alfred Knopf, 1974), p. 246.

16. U.S. Senate, Select Committee to Study Governmental Operations with Respect to Intelligence Activities, Final Report G4-755, 45A (April 26, 1976), pp. 423–471.

17. Ornstein, Susan, "El Salvador: A Mercenary's View," in *Fort Myers' News Press*, October 23, 1983. Interview with former U.S. Marine Lawrence Bailey.

18. McClintock, p. 271.

19. Blum, Willian, *The CIA: A Forgotten History* (London: Zed Books, 1986), p. 271.

Chapter 8

1. Wilkinson, Paul, *Terrorism and the Liberal State*, 2nd ed. (New York: New York University Press, 1986), p. 126.

2. *Ibid.*, pp. 12–19.

3. Willy Brandt, speech to political convention, *New York Times*, September 18, 1977, p. 19.

4. Becker, Jillian, in *Contemporary Terror, Studies in Sub-state Violence*, David Carlton and Carlo Schaerf, ed., (New York: St. Martin's Press, 1981), p. 122.

5. *Ibid.*, p. 132.

6. Wolf, John B., *Fear of Fear: A Survey of Terrorist Operations and Controls in Open Societies* (New York: Plenum Press, 1981), p. 130.

7. *Ibid.*, p. 124.

8. Bell, J. Bowyer, *A Time of Terror: How Democratic Societies Respond to Revolutionary Violence* (New York: Basic Books, 1978), p. 87.

9. Ledeen, Michael, "Visions of Hobnails: European Criticisms of West Germany's Anti-Terrorist Measures," *The New Republic* (November 19, 1977): 17–19.

10. Lasky, Melvin, J., "Ulrike and Andreas: The Bonnie and Clyde of West Germany's Radical Subculture May Have Failed to Make a Revolution But They Have Bruised the Body Politic," *New York Times Magazine* (May 11, 1975): 73.

11. U.S. Senate Select Committee to Study Government Operations with Respect to Intelligence Activities (Church Committee) (September 23, 1975), (44B), p. 142.

12. Church Committee Report, "Findings and Recommendations" (45B), p. 266.

13. Church Committee Report, "The FBI, Domestic Intelligence, and COINTELPRO" (45B), p. 7.

14. Dobson, Christopher, and Ronald Payne, *The Terrorists*, rev. ed. (New York: Facts on File—1982), p. 61.

15. Special Report of the Ad Hoc Interagency Committee on Intelligence, J. Edgar Hoover, Chairman (June 1970), p. 9. Also known as The Huston Plan, in

The Intelligence Community, History Organization, Issues, Tyrus G. Fain, ed. (New York: R. R. Bowker, 1977), p. 832.

16. Parry, Albert, *Terrorism from Robespierre to Arafat* (New York: Vanguard Press, 1977), p. 304.

17. Rosie, George, *The Directory of International Terrorism* (New York: Paragon House, 1986), p. 74.

18. Parry, p. 311.

19. *Ibid.*, p. 317.

20. Wilson, Colin, and Donald Seaman, *The Encyclopedia of Modern Murder, 1962–1982* (New York: Putnam's, 1985), p. 139.

21. *Ibid.*, p. 139.

22. *Ibid.*, p. 140.

23. Church Committee Report, "Findings and Recommendations with Regard to Domestic Intelligence Operations" (45B), p. 266.

24. Fain, Tyrus G., ed., *The Intelligence Community* (New York: R. R. Bowker, 1977), p. xxi.

25. Church Committee Report, "The Scope of Domestic Intelligence" (45B), p. 6.

26. *Ibid.*

27. *Ibid.*

28. Rosie, p. 116.

29. Rockefeller Commission, "Findings," *Report on CIA Activities within the United States, Special Operations Group—"Operation Chaos"* (1975), p. 16.

30. *Ibid.*

31. Church Committee Report, "The Scope of Domestic Intelligence," (45B), p. 6.

32. Hull, Roger, *The Irish Triangle* (Princeton, N.J.: Princeton University Press, 1976), p. 224.

33. Scarman, Sir Leslie, *English Law—The New Dimenson* (London: Stevens, 1974), p. 15.

34. R.U.C. Press Office, Belfast, quoted in Paul Wilkinson, *Terrorism and the Liberal State* (New York: New York University Press, 1986), p. 88.

35. Hull, Roger H., *The Irish Triangle* (Princeton, N.J.: Princeton University Press, 1976), p. 211.

36. McGuffin, John, *Internment* (Tralee, Ireland: Anvil Books, 1973), p. 87.

37. *London Sunday Times* Insight Team, *Northern Ireland: A Report on the Conflict* (London, 1972).

38. Ingraham, Barton L., *Political Crime in Europe,* (Berkeley: University of California Press, 1979), p. 295.

39. *Case of Ireland Against the United Kingdom,* Judgment of the European Court of Human Rights, delivered on January 18, 1978.

40. Committee of Inquiry into Police Interrogation Procedures in Northern Ireland, Judge H. G. Bennett, Q.C., Chairman, *Report* (London: Her Majesty's Stationery Office, 1979), Part III, Chapter 8, Medical Evidence (159), pp. 53–55.

41. *Ibid.*, pt. III, ch. 9, "The Conduct of Interrogations," p. 63.

42. Goldstein, Michael, "Israeli Security Measures in the Occupied Territories," *Middle East Journal* 32 (Winter 1978): 43.

43. Palestinian National Charter, art. 9 (1968).

44. National Lawyers Guild, International Law Subcommittee, *Minority Report on the Treatment of Palestinians in the Israeli Occupied Territories* (N.Y.: 1978).

45. Livingstone, Neil, and Terrell Arnold, *Fighting Back* (Lexington, Mass.: D.C. Heath, 1984), p. 203.

46. Alon, Hanon, *Countering Palestinian Terrorism in Israel* (Santa Monica, Calif.: RAND Corp., 1986), p. viii.

47. *Ibid.*, p. 70.

48. *London Sunday Times* Insight Report, June 19, 1977.

49. Goldstein, p. 44.

50. *Ibid.*

51. *Ibid.*

52. Benvenisti, Meron, *The West Bank Data Project 1986 Report* (Washington, D.C.: American Enterprise Institute, 1986), p. 43.

53. Goldstein, p. 35.

54. Benvenisti, p. 41.

55. *Human Rights in the Administered Territories* (Washington, D.C.: Embassy of Israel, 1978), p. 5.

56. *London Sunday Times, op cit.*

57. National Lawyers Guild, p. 4.

58. Benvenisti, p. 44.

Chapter 9

1. Carlton, David, and Carlo Schaerf, eds., *International Terrorism and World Security* (New York: Wiley, 1975), p. 73.

2. U.N. General Assembly, "Report of the International Law Commission on the Work of Its Sixth Committee," Supplement 2 (A/26-93), *YBILC*, vol. II, (1954), p. 112.

3. U.N. General Assembly, "Report of the Special Committee on the Question of Defining Aggression," 25 UN DOC. A/8028 (1970), no. 28 p. 121.

4. U.N. General Assembly Resolution 2625 (XXIV, Declaration on Principles of International Law Concerning Friendly Relations and Cooperation among States in Accordance with the Charter of the United Nations (October 24, 1970).

5. Evans, Alona, and John Murphy, *Legal Aspects of International Terrorism* (Lexington, Mass.: D.C. Heath, 1978), p. 5.

6. Murphy, John, *Punishing International Terrorists* (Totowa, N.J.: Rowman and Allenheld, 1985), p. 115.

7. Evans and Murphy, p. 68.

8. Abraham Sofaer, legal adviser to the United States Department of State, Testimony before the U.S. Senate Foreign Relations Committee, (August 1, 1985).

Recommended Readings

Martha Crenshaw, ed., *Terrorism, Legitimacy and Power: The Consequence of Political Violence* (Middletown, CT.: Wesleyan University Press, 1983).

Kevin Kelley, *The Longest War: Northern Ireland and the IRA* (Westport, CT.: Lawrence Hill & Company, 1932).

Walter Laqueur, *Terrorism* (Boston: Little, Brown and Company, 1977).

Carlos Marighella, *The Terrorist Classic: Manual of the Urban Guerrilla* (Chapel Hill, N.C.: Documentary Publications, 1985).

Benjamin Netanyahu, ed., *Terrorism: How the West Can Win* (NY: Farrar, Straus and Giroux, 1986).

Conor Cruise O'Brien, *The Siege: The Saga of Israel and Zionism* (NY: Simon & Schuster, 1986).

Paul Wilkinson, *Terrorism and the Liberal State*, 2nd edition (New York: New York University Press, 1986).

Index

About the Author

Donna M. Schlagheck received her Ph.D. from the University of Minnesota. She is an Assistant Professor of Political Science at Wright State University in Dayton, Ohio, where she lectures on international conflict and American foreign policy. A native of Cincinnati, Donna Schlagheck encountered terrorism first-hand while studying abroad, when plans to attend the Munich Olympic Games in 1972 were altered by zealous German border guards. She has been studying the Palestinians and other cases of international terrorism since that time, and teaches a seminar on the subject once a year. That seminar led her to write this book, introducing her students to the many fascinating faces of terrorism. She is a member of the American Political Science Association, International Studies Association, Dayton Council on World Affairs, and Phi Beta Kappa.